Soups

101 recipes

Publications International, Ltd.

Pictured on the front cover: Creamy Tuscan Bean & Chicken Soup *(page 60)*.
Pictured on the back cover *(from left):* Minestrone alla Milanese *(page 58)* and Black Bean Vegetarian Chili *(page 91)*.

ISBN-13: 978-1-4508-2162-9
ISBN-10: 1-4508-2162-6

Library of Congress Control Number: 2011921192

Manufactured in China.

8 7 6 5 4 3 2 1

Microwave Cooking: Microwave ovens vary in wattage. Use the cooking times as guidelines and check for doneness before adding more time.

Preparation/Cooking Times: Preparation times are based on the approximate amount of time required to assemble the recipe before cooking, baking, chilling or serving. These times include preparation steps such as measuring, chopping and mixing. The fact that some preparations and cooking can be done simultaneously is taken into account. Preparation of optional ingredients and serving suggestions is not included.

Publications International, Ltd.

table of contents

split pea soup
page 9

hearty vegetable pasta soup
page 117

grandma ruth's minestrone
makes 4 servings

- 1 pound ground beef
- 1 can (about 15 ounces) red beans, rinsed and drained
- 1 package (16 ounces) frozen mixed vegetables
- 2 cans (8 ounces each) tomato sauce
- 1 can (about 14 ounces) diced tomatoes
- 1/4 head shredded cabbage (about 2 cups)
- 1 cup chopped onions
- 1 cup chopped celery
- 1/2 cup chopped fresh Italian parsley
- 1 tablespoon dried basil
- 1 tablespoon Italian seasoning
- 1 teaspoon salt
- 1 teaspoon black pepper
- 1 cup cooked macaroni

slow cooker directions

1. Brown beef in large skillet over medium-high heat 6 to 8 minutes, stirring to break up meat. Drain fat.

2. Combine beef and beans in slow cooker. Cover; cook on HIGH 2 hours.

3. *Turn slow cooker to LOW.* Stir in vegetables, tomato sauce, tomatoes, cabbage, onions, celery, parsley, basil, seasoning, salt and pepper. Cover; cook 6 to 8 hours.

4. *Turn slow cooker to HIGH.* Stir in macaroni. Cover; cook 30 minutes.

corn chowder with smoked sausage

makes 6 to 8 servings

    1 package HILLSHIRE FARM® Smoked Sausage
¼ cup butter or margarine
    1 medium onion, chopped (about 1 cup)
¼ cup all-purpose flour
½ teaspoon salt
⅛ teaspoon ground black pepper
    4 cups milk
    1 can (15¼ ounces) whole kernel corn, drained
    2 cups cubed potatoes, cooked, drained
      Chopped parsley and shredded Cheddar cheese (optional)

1. Cut sausage into ½-inch cubes.

2. Melt butter in large saucepan over medium heat. Add onion; cook and stir until tender. Add flour, salt and pepper; cook, stirring constantly, 1 minute. Add milk.

3. Increase heat to medium-high and bring to a boil, stirring constantly.

4. Boil and stir 1 minute. Add corn and sausage; return to a boil. Reduce heat to medium-low and simmer 10 minutes. Stir in potatoes; heat through.

5. Top each serving with parsley and cheese, if desired.

thick and creamy succotash soup

makes 6 servings

2 strips bacon
1 onion, chopped
1 stalk celery, chopped
2 tablespoons all-purpose flour
3 cups chicken broth
1½ cups corn
1 cup frozen baby lima beans, thawed
1 bay leaf
¼ teaspoon salt
¼ teaspoon black pepper
¼ teaspoon hot pepper sauce
½ cup whipping cream

1. Cook bacon in Dutch oven over medium heat until crisp. Drain on paper towels. Crumble and set aside.

2. Add onion and celery to bacon drippings in Dutch oven; cook and stir 5 minutes or until tender. Stir in flour; cook until slightly thickened. Stir in broth. Bring to a boil over high heat. Reduce heat to low; simmer until slightly thickened.

3. Stir in bacon, corn, beans, bay leaf, salt, black pepper and hot pepper sauce; simmer 15 minutes. Remove from heat; stir in cream. Remove and discard bay leaf before serving.

potluck tip: If preparing in advance, cover and refrigerate up to one day. To serve at your host's home, reheat over low heat. (Do not allow soup to boil.) If you prepare it the same day, wrap covered Dutch oven in several layers of aluminum foil and overwrap with thick towel or newspapers to keep the finished dish warm when transporting.

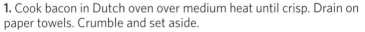

split pea soup

makes 6 servings

- **1 package (16 ounces) dried green or yellow split peas**
- **7 cups water**
- **1 pound smoked ham hocks *or* 4 ounces smoked sausage links, sliced and quartered**
- **2 carrots, chopped**
- **1 onion, chopped**
- **¾ teaspoon salt**
- **½ teaspoon dried basil**
- **¼ teaspoon dried oregano**
- **¼ teaspoon black pepper**

1. Rinse peas thoroughly in colander under cold running water; discard any debris or blemished peas.

2. Combine peas, water, ham hocks, carrots, onion, salt, basil, oregano and pepper in Dutch oven. Bring to a boil over high heat. Reduce heat to low; simmer 1 hour 15 minutes or until tender, stirring occasionally. Stir frequently near end of cooking to keep soup from scorching.

3. Remove ham hocks; let stand until cool enough to handle. Remove ham from hocks; chop. Discard bones.

4. Place 3 cups soup in food processor or blender; process until smooth.

5. Return to Dutch oven; stir in ham. Cook just until heated through.

bacon potato chowder

makes 8 servings

    4 slices bacon, cooked and crumbled
    1 large onion, chopped (about 1 cup)
    4 cans (10¾ ounces each) CAMPBELL'S® Condensed Cream of
        Potato Soup
    4 soup cans milk
    ¼ teaspoon ground black pepper
    2 large russet potatoes, cut into ½-inch pieces (about 3 cups)
    ½ cup chopped fresh chives
    2 cups shredded Cheddar cheese (about 8 ounces)

slow cooker directions

1. Stir the bacon, onion, soup, milk, black pepper, potatoes and ¼ cup chives in a 6-quart slow cooker.

2. Cover and cook on HIGH for 3 to 4 hours or until the potatoes are tender.

3. Add the cheese and stir until the cheese is melted. Serve with the remaining chives.

prep time: 15 minutes • **cook time:** 3 to 4 hours

tip: One of the most readily available potato varieties is the russet, also known as Idaho or baking potatoes. They are long with slightly rounded ends and rough brown skin.

louisiana gumbo
makes 6 servings

2 cups **MINUTE®** White Rice, uncooked
2 tablespoons butter
2 tablespoons all-purpose flour
½ cup onion, chopped
½ cup celery, chopped
½ cup green bell pepper, chopped
1 clove garlic, minced
1 package (14 ounces) smoked turkey sausage, sliced
1 can (14½ ounces) diced tomatoes
1 can (14½ ounces) chicken broth
1 package (10 ounces) frozen sliced okra, thawed*
1 tablespoon Cajun seasoning
¼ teaspoon dried thyme
½ pound shrimp, peeled and deveined
Salt and black pepper

*Or substitute 1 package (10 ounces) frozen cut green beans.

Prepare rice according to package directions.

Melt butter in large skillet over medium-high heat. Stir in flour; cook and stir until light golden brown, about 5 minutes. Add onion, celery, bell pepper and garlic; cook 2 to 3 minutes or until tender.

Stir in sausage, tomatoes, broth, okra, seasoning and thyme; cover. Simmer 5 minutes, stirring occasionally.

Add shrimp; cook 5 minutes or until shrimp are pink. Season with salt and pepper to taste. Serve with rice.

chicken and homemade noodle soup

makes 4 servings

3/4 cup all-purpose flour
2 teaspoons finely chopped fresh thyme, divided
1/4 teaspoon salt
1 egg yolk, beaten
2 cups plus 3 tablespoons cold water, divided
1 pound boneless skinless chicken thighs, cut into 1/2- to 3/4-inch pieces
5 cups chicken broth
1 onion, chopped
1 carrot, thinly sliced
3/4 cup frozen peas
Chopped fresh Italian parsley

1. Stir together flour, 1 teaspoon thyme and salt in small bowl. Add egg yolk and 3 tablespoons water; stir until mixed. Shape into small ball. Place dough on lightly floured surface; flatten slightly. Knead 5 minutes or until dough is smooth and elastic, adding more flour to prevent sticking, if necessary. Cover with plastic wrap. Let stand 15 minutes.

2. Roll out dough to 1/8-inch thickness on lightly floured surface. If dough is too elastic, let rest several minutes. Let dough stand 30 minutes to dry slightly. Cut into 1/4-inch-wide strips. Cut strips 1 1/2 to 2 inches long.

3. Combine chicken and remaining 2 cups water in large saucepan. Bring to a boil over high heat. Reduce heat to low; cover and simmer 5 minutes or until chicken is cooked through. Drain well.

4. Combine broth, onion, carrot and remaining 1 teaspoon thyme in saucepan. Bring to a boil over high heat. Add noodles. Reduce heat to low; simmer, uncovered, 8 minutes or until noodles are tender. Stir in chicken and peas; simmer until heated through. Sprinkle with parsley just before serving.

tomato soup
makes 6 servings

1 tablespoon vegetable oil
1 cup chopped onion
2 cloves garlic, coarsely chopped
½ cup chopped carrot
¼ cup chopped celery
2 cans (28 ounces each) crushed tomatoes in tomato purée
3½ cups chicken broth
1 tablespoon Worcestershire sauce
½ to 1 teaspoon salt
½ teaspoon dried thyme
¼ to ½ teaspoon black pepper
2 to 4 drops hot pepper sauce

1. Heat oil in large saucepan or Dutch oven over medium-high heat. Add onion and garlic; cook and stir 1 to 2 minutes or until onion is soft. Add carrot and celery; cook 7 to 9 minutes or until tender, stirring occasionally.

2. Stir in tomatoes, broth, Worcestershire sauce, salt, thyme, black pepper and hot pepper sauce. Reduce heat to low; cover and simmer 20 minutes, stirring occasionally.

3. For smoother soup, remove from heat. Let cool about 10 minutes. Working in batches, process soup in food processor or blender until smooth. Return soup to Dutch oven; simmer 3 to 5 minutes or until heated through.

brunswick stew

makes 6 to 8 servings

1 whole chicken (about 4 pounds), cut up
2 quarts water
1 stalk celery (including leaves), cut into
    2-inch pieces
1 onion, quartered
1 clove garlic, halved
2 teaspoons salt
1 teaspoon whole black peppercorns
1 can (about 14 ounces) diced tomatoes
2 russet potatoes, peeled and cubed
1 onion, thinly sliced
¼ cup tomato paste
1 teaspoon sugar
½ teaspoon *each* ground black pepper and dried thyme
⅛ teaspoon garlic powder
    Dash hot pepper sauce
1 package (10 ounces) frozen lima beans
1 package (10 ounces) frozen corn

1. Place chicken and water in Dutch oven; bring to a boil over medium-high heat. Skim off foam. Add celery, quartered onion, garlic, salt and peppercorns; return to a boil. Reduce heat to low; cover and simmer 2½ hours or until chicken is cooked through.

2. Remove chicken from broth; cool slightly. Remove meat, discarding skin and bones. Cut enough chicken into 1-inch pieces to measure 3 cups. (Reserve remaining chicken for another use.)

3. Strain broth through double thickness of cheesecloth. Discard vegetables; skim off fat. Return 1 quart broth to Dutch oven. (Reserve remaining broth for another use.)

4. Add tomatoes, potatoes, sliced onion, tomato paste, sugar, ground black pepper, thyme, garlic powder and hot pepper sauce; bring to a boil over medium-high heat. Reduce heat to low; cover and simmer 30 minutes. Add beans and corn; simmer, covered, 5 minutes. Add chicken; cook 5 minutes or until heated through.

carrot soup
makes 4 servings

2 teaspoons butter
⅓ cup chopped onion
1 tablespoon chopped fresh ginger
1 pound baby carrots
½ teaspoon salt
¼ teaspoon black pepper
3 cups vegetable broth
¼ cup whipping cream
¼ cup orange juice
Pinch ground nutmeg
4 tablespoons sour cream

1. Melt butter in large saucepan over medium-high heat. Add onion and ginger; cook and stir 1 minute or until ginger is fragrant. Add carrots, salt and pepper; cook and stir 2 minutes.

2. Stir in broth; bring to a boil. Reduce heat to low; cover and simmer 30 minutes or until carrots are tender.

3. Working in batches, process soup in blender or food processor until smooth. Return to saucepan; stir in cream, orange juice and nutmeg. Cook over medium heat until heated through, stirring occasionally. Thin soup with additional broth, if necessary. Top with sour cream just before serving.

oven-roasted onion soup
makes 4 servings

- ¼ cup (½ stick) butter
- 3 yellow onions, thinly sliced
- 1 teaspoon salt
- ½ teaspoon freshly ground pepper
- 6 cups reduced-sodium beef broth
- ½ cup brewed coffee
- ¼ cup dry sherry
- 1 baguette, cut into ½-inch slices
- 1 cup grated Swiss cheese
- 6 small sprigs thyme (optional)

1. Preheat oven to 325°F. Melt butter in Dutch oven over medium heat. Add onions, salt and pepper; cook and stir 10 minutes or until onions are golden but not browned. Cover and bake 45 minutes, stirring once.

2. Stir in broth; cover and bake 30 minutes. Remove from oven; stir in coffee and sherry. Bring to a simmer over medium heat. Remove from heat.

3. Place bread slices on baking sheet. Bake until lightly browned on both sides, turning once.

4. Preheat broiler and ladle soup into four ovenproof bowls. Top each serving with toast and 1 tablespoon Swiss cheese.

5. Place bowls in large baking pan; broil 2 to 3 minutes or until cheese is melted. Garnish with thyme.

roasted corn and chicken soup

makes 8 servings

- 4 tablespoons olive oil, divided
- 1 can (15 ounces) yellow corn, drained
- 1 can (15 ounces) white corn, drained
- 1 onion, diced
- 3 tablespoons ORTEGA® Fire-Roasted Diced Green Chiles
- ½ of 1½- to 2-pound cooked rotisserie chicken, bones removed and meat shredded
- 1 packet (1.25 ounces) ORTEGA® 40% Less Sodium Taco Seasoning Mix
- 4 cups chicken broth
- 4 ORTEGA® Yellow Corn Taco Shells, crumbled

Heat 2 tablespoons oil over medium heat in large skillet until hot. Add corn. Cook 8 minutes or until browned; stir often to prevent corn from burning. Add remaining 2 tablespoons oil, onion and chiles. Cook and stir 3 minutes longer.

Transfer mixture to large pot. Stir in shredded chicken. Add seasoning mix and toss to combine. Stir in chicken broth and bring to a boil. Reduce heat to low. Simmer 15 minutes. Serve with crumbled taco shells.

note: To make sure the canned corn is well drained, press excess water out with a paper towel.

prep time: 15 minutes • **start-to-finish time:** 30 minutes

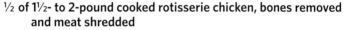

hamburger veggie soup
makes 4 to 6 servings

1 pound ground beef
1 bag (16 ounces) frozen mixed vegetables
1 package (10 ounces) frozen seasoning
    blend vegetables
1 can (about 14 ounces) stewed tomatoes,
    undrained
2 cans (5½ ounces each) spicy vegetable
    juice
1 can (10¾ ounces) condensed tomato soup, undiluted
Salt and black pepper

slow cooker directions

1. Brown beef in large skillet over medium-high heat 6 to 8 minutes, stirring to break up meat. Drain fat.

2. Combine beef, vegetables, tomatoes, juice and soup in slow cooker. Stir well.

3. Cover; cook on HIGH 4 hours. Season with salt and pepper.

prep time: 5 minutes • **cook time:** 4 hours

tip: Frozen seasoning blend vegetables are a combination of vegetables such as celery, bell peppers, onions and occasionally parsley.

harvest soup
makes 6 to 8 servings

- ½ pound BOB EVANS® Special Seasonings Roll Sausage
- 1 large onion, finely chopped
- 2½ cups chicken broth
- 2 cups canned pumpkin
- 2 cups hot milk
- 1 teaspoon lemon juice
- Dash ground nutmeg
- Dash ground cinnamon
- Salt and black pepper
- Chopped fresh parsley

Crumble and cook sausage and onion in large saucepan until sausage is browned. Drain off any drippings.

Add broth and bring to a boil. Stir in pumpkin; cover and simmer over low heat 15 to 20 minutes.

Add milk, lemon juice, nutmeg, cinnamon, salt and pepper; simmer, uncovered, 5 minutes to blend flavors.

Sprinkle with parsley before serving. Refrigerate leftovers.

matzo ball soup
makes 6 servings

- **4 eggs**
- **1 cup matzo meal**
- **¼ cup (½ stick) butter, melted and cooled**
- **2 tablespoons water**
- **1 tablespoon grated raw onion**
- **½ teaspoon salt**
- **⅛ teaspoon white pepper** *or* **¼ teaspoon black pepper**
- **2 quarts chicken broth**
- **Chopped fresh Italian parsley (optional)**

1. Beat eggs in large bowl with electric mixer at medium speed. Add matzo meal, butter, water, onion, salt and pepper; beat at low speed until well blended. Let stand 15 to 30 minutes. With wet hands, form mixture into 12 (2-inch) balls.

2. Bring 8 cups water to a boil in Dutch oven. Drop matzo balls, one at a time, into boiling water. Reduce heat to low; cover and simmer 35 minutes or until cooked through. Remove from Dutch oven; drain well. Discard water.

3. Bring broth to a boil over high heat in same Dutch oven. Add matzo balls. Reduce heat to low; simmer, covered, 5 minutes or until matzo balls are heated through. Garnish with parsley.

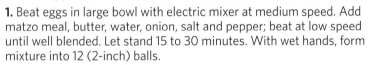

two-cheese potato and cauliflower soup

makes 4 to 6 servings

- **1 tablespoon butter**
- **1 cup chopped onion**
- **2 cloves garlic, minced**
- **5 cups whole milk**
- **1 pound Yukon Gold potatoes, diced**
- **1 pound cauliflower florets**
- **1½ teaspoons salt**
- **⅛ teaspoon ground red pepper**
- **1½ cups (6 ounces) shredded sharp Cheddar cheese**
- **⅓ cup crumbled blue cheese**

1. Melt butter in large saucepan over medium-high heat. Add onion; cook and stir 4 minutes or until translucent. Add garlic; cook and stir 15 seconds. Add milk, potatoes, cauliflower, salt and red pepper; bring to a boil. Reduce heat to low; cover and simmer 15 minutes or until potatoes are tender. Cool slightly.

2. Working in batches, process soup in blender or food processor until smooth. Return to saucepan. Cook and stir over medium heat just until heated through. Remove from heat; add cheeses. Stir until cheeses are melted.

tip: One pound of trimmed cauliflower will yield about 1½ cups of florets. You can also substitute 1 pound of frozen cauliflower florets for the fresh florets.

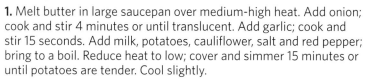

cajun shrimp and potato chowder
makes 4 servings

- **1 tablespoon olive oil**
- **½ pound medium shrimp (26 to 30 count), peeled, deveined (thawed if frozen)**
- **½ cup chopped onion**
- **½ cup chopped green bell pepper**
- **2 cups SIMPLY POTATOES® Homestyle Slices, chopped slightly**
- **1 can (14 ounces) chicken broth**
- **2 teaspoons Cajun seasoning**
- **2 tablespoons all-purpose flour**
- **2 tablespoons water**
- **1 can (14½ ounces) diced tomatoes, undrained**

1. Heat oil in 2-quart saucepan over medium heat. Add shrimp, onion and green pepper. Cook, stirring occasionally, until shrimp are pink. Add SIMPLY POTATOES®, broth and Cajun seasoning. Bring to a boil. Reduce heat to low. Cook, stirring occasionally, until SIMPLY POTATOES® are tender (20 to 25 minutes).

2. In small bowl, combine flour and water; stir until smooth. Add flour mixture to soup. Stir in tomatoes. Cook until mixture is thickened and heated through.

total time: 35 minutes

roasted chicken with caramelized onions soup

makes 6 servings

- **2 teaspoons vegetable oil**
- **2 medium onions, halved and thinly sliced (about 1 cup)**
- **8 cups SWANSON® Chicken Broth (Regular, Natural Goodness® or Certified Organic)**
- **⅛ teaspoon ground black pepper**
- **2 medium carrots, sliced (about 1 cup)**
- **2 stalks celery, sliced (about 1 cup)**
- **¾ cup uncooked trumpet-shaped pasta (campanelle)**
- **2 cups shredded roasted chicken**

1. Heat the oil in a 10-inch skillet over medium-high heat. Add the onions and cook until they begin to brown, stirring occasionally. Reduce the heat to medium. Cook until the onions are tender and caramelized, stirring occasionally. Remove the skillet from the heat.

2. Heat the broth, pepper, carrots and celery in a 4-quart saucepan over medium-high heat to a boil. Stir the pasta and chicken into the saucepan. Reduce heat to medium and cook for 10 minutes or until the pasta is tender. Stir in the onions and serve immediately.

kitchen tip: Cut the peeled onions in half lengthwise. Place the halves cut-side down on the cutting surface. Slice each onion half with parallel cuts up to, but not through, the root. Cut the root end off to free the slices.

prep time: 10 minutes • **cook time:** 30 minutes

curried sweet potato and carrot soup
makes 8 servings

  **2 sweet potatoes, peeled and cut into
      ³/₄-inch cubes (about 5 cups)**
  2 cups baby carrots
  1 onion, chopped
  ³/₄ teaspoon curry powder
  ¹/₂ teaspoon salt
  ¹/₂ teaspoon black pepper
  ¹/₂ teaspoon ground cinnamon
  ¹/₄ teaspoon ground ginger
  4 cups chicken broth
  ³/₄ cup half-and-half
  1 tablespoon maple syrup
  Candied ginger (optional)

slow cooker directions

1. Combine sweet potatoes, carrots, onion, curry powder, salt, pepper, cinnamon and ground ginger in slow cooker. Pour in broth. Cover; cook on LOW 7 to 8 hours.

2. Working in batches, process soup in blender or food processor until smooth. Return to slow cooker. (Or use immersion blender.) Add half-and-half and maple syrup. Cover; cook on HIGH 15 minutes or until heated through. Garnish with candied ginger.

prep time: 10 minutes • **cook time:** 7 to 8 hours

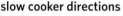

california fish stew

makes 10 to 12 servings

  3 cups Zinfandel or other dry red wine, divided
  1 quart mussels, cleaned*
¼ cup olive oil
  1 package (8 ounces) mushrooms, sliced
  1 green bell pepper, chopped
  1 onion, chopped
  2 cloves garlic, minced
  1 can (about 28 ounces) whole Italian plum tomatoes,
     undrained
¼ cup tomato paste
  1 teaspoon salt
½ teaspoon black pepper
  3 pounds striped bass or other firm fish fillets, cut into
     bite-size pieces
  2 tablespoons finely chopped fresh basil
  1 pound crabmeat**
  1 pound medium raw shrimp, peeled
  3 tablespoons chopped fresh Italian parsley

*Discard mussels that stay open when tapped with your fingers. To clean mussels, scrub
with stiff brush under cold running water. To debeard, pull threads from shells.

**Pick out and discard any shell or cartilage from crabmeat.

1. Bring 1 cup wine to a boil in large Dutch oven. Add mussels; cover
and reduce heat to low. Steam 5 to 7 minutes or until shells open.
Transfer to large bowl with slotted spoon. (Discard any unopened
shells.) Strain cooking liquid through cheesecloth and reserve.

2. Heat oil in same Dutch oven. Add mushrooms, bell pepper, onion
and garlic; cook and stir 3 minutes. Add tomatoes; cook 4 minutes.
Stir in reserved cooking liquid, tomato paste and remaining 2 cups
wine. Add salt and pepper; simmer 20 minutes.

3. Add fish and basil; cook 5 minutes or until fish begins to flake when
tested with fork. Add mussels, crabmeat and shrimp. Cook 3 minutes
or until shrimp are pink and opaque, stirring occasionally. Sprinkle
with parsley; serve immediately.

coconut curry chicken soup

makes 4 servings

3 cups chicken broth
8 boneless skinless chicken thighs
1 cup chopped onion, divided
1 teaspoon salt, divided
4 whole cloves
1 tablespoon butter
2 tablespoons curry powder
1¼ cups coconut milk
¼ cup plus 1 tablespoon chopped fresh mint, divided
3 tablespoons crystallized ginger
¼ teaspoon ground cloves
1½ cups half-and-half
3 cups cooked rice (optional)
Lime wedges (optional)

1. Bring broth to a boil in large saucepan over high heat. Add chicken, ½ cup onion, ½ teaspoon salt and whole cloves. Return to a boil. Reduce heat to low; cover and simmer 40 minutes or until tender.

2. Remove chicken; set aside. Reserve 1 cup cooking liquid; discard remaining liquid, onion and cloves. Increase heat to medium-high; melt butter in saucepan. Add remaining ½ cup onion; cook and stir 4 minutes or until translucent. Sprinkle curry powder over onions; cook and stir just until fragrant.

3. Add coconut milk, 1 tablespoon mint, ginger, ground cloves and reserved cooking liquid to saucepan. Cover; simmer 10 minutes. Add chicken; cover and simmer 15 minutes. Stir in half-and-half and remaining ½ teaspoon salt. Shred chicken, pressing down with spoon. Cook 1 minute or until heated through. Sprinkle with remaining ¼ cup mint. Serve with rice and lime wedges, if desired.

spicy peanut soup
makes 8 servings

- 2 tablespoons vegetable oil
- 2 large onions, diced (about 2 cups)
- 2 large carrots, diced (about 1 cup)
- 1 tablespoon minced fresh ginger root
- ¼ teaspoon ground red pepper
- 6 cups SWANSON® Chicken Broth (Regular, Natural Goodness® or Certified Organic)
- 2 large sweet potatoes, peeled and diced (about 3 cups)
- 1 cup creamy peanut butter
- ⅓ cup sliced green onion or chives
- ⅓ cup chopped peanuts

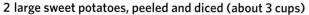

1. Heat the oil in a 4-quart saucepot over medium heat. Add the onions, carrots and ginger and cook until they're tender-crisp. Add the red pepper and cook for 1 minute.

2. Stir the broth and sweet potatoes in the saucepot. Heat to a boil. Reduce the heat to low. Cover and cook for 20 minutes or until the vegetables are tender. Stir in the peanut butter.

3. Place one third of the broth mixture in a blender or food processor. Cover and blend until smooth. Pour into a large bowl. Repeat the blending process twice more with the remaining broth mixture. Return all of the puréed mixture to the saucepot. Cook over medium heat until the mixture is hot. Season to taste. Divide the soup among 8 serving bowls. Top each serving of soup with the green onions and peanuts.

prep time: 15 minutes • **cook time:** 30 minutes

cream of roasted fennel soup

makes 8 servings

3 fennel bulbs, cut into ½-inch slices
2 large onions, cut into ½-inch slices (about 2 cups)
2 cloves garlic, minced
¼ teaspoon cracked black pepper
2 tablespoons olive oil
5¼ cups SWANSON® Vegetable Broth
(Regular or Certified Organic)
½ cup heavy cream
¼ cup coarsely chopped fresh basil leaves

1. Heat the oven to 425°F. Place the fennel, onions, garlic and black pepper into a 17×11-inch roasting pan. Pour the oil over the vegetables and toss to coat. Bake for 30 minutes or until the vegetables are tender.

2. Place half of the vegetables and 1 cup of the broth in a food processor. Cover and blend until the mixture is smooth. Pour the vegetable mixture into a 4-quart saucepan. Repeat with the remaining vegetables and 1 cup of the broth.

3. Stir the remaining broth, cream and basil in the saucepan and heat over medium heat to a boil. Reduce the heat to low. Cook for 10 minutes, stirring occasionally. Season to taste with additional black pepper.

prep time: 10 minutes • **cook time:** 40 minutes

celery-leek bisque with basil

makes 4 to 6 servings

3 bunches leeks (3 pounds), trimmed and
    well rinsed*
2 cans (about 14 ounces each) chicken
    broth
2 stalks celery, sliced
1 carrot, peeled and sliced (3 ounces)
3 cloves garlic, minced
1 cup cream cheese with garlic and herbs
2 cups half-and-half, plus additional for garnish
    Salt and black pepper
    Fresh basil leaves (optional)

*Thoroughly rinsing the leeks is very important. Gritty sand can get between the layers of the leeks and can be difficult to see, so you may need to rinse them several times.

slow cooker directions

1. Combine leeks, broth, celery, carrot and garlic in slow cooker. Cover; cook on LOW 8 hours or on HIGH 4 hours.

2. Working in batches, process soup in blender or food processor until smooth. Add cream cheese to last batch.

3. Return to slow cooker. Stir in half-and-half. Season with salt and pepper. For best flavor, cool to room temperature; refrigerate overnight. Reheat in large saucepan over medium heat before serving. Garnish with swirl of half-and-half and basil.

prep time: 45 minutes • **cook time:** 8 hours (LOW) or 4 hours (HIGH)

potato soup with arugula
makes 6 servings

- **2 tablespoons olive oil**
- **2 leeks, white parts only, cleaned and chopped**
- **4 medium potatoes, peeled and diced**
- **3 cups SWANSON® Chicken Broth (Regular, Natural Goodness® or Certified Organic)**
- **1 cup baby arugula**
- **¼ cup heavy cream**
- **2 teaspoons lemon juice**

1. Heat the oil in a 4-quart saucepan over medium heat. Add the leeks and cook for 5 minutes. Add the potatoes and cook for 10 minutes or until the potatoes are almost tender.

2. Add the broth. Heat to a boil. Reduce the heat to low. Cover and cook for 20 minutes or until the potatoes are tender. Add the arugula. Cook for 1 minute.

3. Place half of the broth mixture into an electric blender or food processor container. Cover and blend until smooth. Pour the mixture into a medium bowl. Repeat the blending process with the remaining broth mixture. Return all of the puréed mixture to the saucepan. Cook over medium heat until the mixture is hot. Season to taste. Stir in the cream and lemon juice. Serve immediately.

kitchen tip: This savory soup is also delicious served cold. Refrigerate for at least 3 hours or until well chilled.

prep time: 15 minutes • **cook time:** 35 minutes

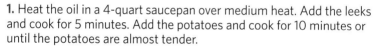

sweet potato bisque

makes 4 servings

    1 pound sweet potatoes, peeled and cut into chunks
    2 teaspoons butter
  ½ cup finely chopped onion
    1 teaspoon curry powder
  ½ teaspoon ground coriander
  ¼ teaspoon salt
  ⅔ cup apple juice
    1 cup buttermilk
  ¼ cup water
    Fresh snipped chives (optional)

1. Place sweet potatoes in large saucepan; cover with water. Bring to a boil over high heat. Cook 15 minutes or until potatoes are fork-tender. Drain; cool under cold running water.

2. Meanwhile, melt butter in small saucepan over medium heat. Add onion; cook and stir 2 minutes. Stir in curry powder, coriander and salt; cook and stir 1 minute or until onion is tender. Remove from heat; stir in apple juice.

3. Combine sweet potatoes, buttermilk and onion mixture in food processor or blender; process until smooth. Return to saucepan; stir in ¼ cup water, if necessary, to thin to desired consistency. Cook and stir over medium heat until heated through. (Do not boil.) Garnish with chives.

corn and crab gazpacho
makes 4 to 6 servings

- 1 cucumber, peeled, seeded and coarsely chopped
- 3 green onions, coarsely chopped
- 2 tablespoons coarsely chopped fresh Italian parsley or cilantro
- 2 pounds grape or cherry tomatoes
- 1 cup cooked fresh corn (1 large ear) *or* 1 cup thawed frozen corn
- 3 cups tomato juice, chilled
- 3 tablespoons olive oil
- 2 tablespoons red wine vinegar
- 1¼ teaspoons red pepper flakes
- 1 teaspoon salt
- ¼ teaspoon black pepper
- 1½ cups flaked cooked crabmeat* *or* 8 ounces cooked baby shrimp

Pick out and discard any shell or cartilage from crabmeat.

1. Combine cucumber, green onions and parsley in food processor. Process using on/off pulsing action until finely chopped. Transfer to large pitcher or bowl. Add tomatoes to food processor. Process using on/off pulsing action until finely chopped. Add to cucumber mixture.

2. Stir corn into pitcher. Add tomato juice, oil, vinegar, red pepper flakes, salt and black pepper. Stir well. Cover; refrigerate 1 to 3 hours.

3. Pour gazpacho into bowls; top with crabmeat.

note: Gazpacho can be made several hours in advance and chilled. Bring to room temperature before serving.

shrimp bisque
makes 6 servings

1 pound medium raw shrimp, peeled and deveined
½ cup chopped onion
½ cup chopped celery
½ cup chopped carrot
2 tablespoons butter or margarine
2 cans (14 ounces each) chicken broth
1 can (14½ ounces) DEL MONTE® Original Recipe Stewed Tomatoes, undrained
¼ teaspoon dried thyme
1 cup half-and-half

1. Cut shrimp into small pieces; set aside. In large saucepan, cook onion, celery and carrot in butter until onion is tender.

2. Add shrimp; cook 1 minute. Add broth, tomatoes and thyme; simmer 10 minutes.

3. Ladle one third of soup into blender container or food processor. Cover and process until smooth. Repeat with remaining soup. Return to saucepan. Add half-and-half. Heat through. (Do not boil.)

variation: Substitute 2 cans (6 ounces each) of crab for shrimp.

prep time: 15 minutes • **cook time:** 20 minutes

oyster stew
makes 8 servings

   1 **quart shucked oysters, with their liquor**
   8 **cups milk**
   8 **tablespoons margarine, cut into pieces**
   1 **teaspoon ground white pepper**
  ½ **teaspoon salt**
     Paprika
   2 **tablespoons finely chopped fresh parsley**

Heat oysters in their liquor in medium saucepan over high heat until oyster edges begin to curl, about 2 to 3 minutes. Heat milk and margarine together in large saucepan over medium-high heat just to boiling. Add pepper and salt.

Stir in oysters and their liquor. Do not boil or overcook stew or oysters may get tough. Pour stew into tureen. Dust with paprika; sprinkle with parsley.

Favorite recipe from **National Fisheries Institute**

tip: When purchasing shucked oysters, look for ones that are plump, uniform in size and have good color. The liquor (liquid) should be clear and they should smell like the sea. Shucked oysters can be stored, covered by their liquor, for up to 2 days in the refrigerator or up to 3 months in the freezer.

zucchini soup with herbed cream

makes 6 servings

½ cup sour cream
4 teaspoons chopped fresh basil leaves
4 teaspoons chopped fresh oregano leaves
2 tablespoons olive oil
1 large onion, finely chopped (about 1 cup)
1 clove garlic, minced
4 medium zucchini, thinly sliced (about 6 cups)
¼ teaspoon ground black pepper
3 cups SWANSON® Vegetable Broth
   (Regular or Certified Organic)

1. Stir the sour cream, 1 teaspoon of the basil and 1 teaspoon of the oregano in a small bowl. Cover and refrigerate.

2. Heat the oil in a 4-quart saucepan over medium heat. Add the onion and garlic and cook until they're tender. Add the zucchini and black pepper. Cook for 5 minutes or until the zucchini is tender.

3. Add the broth, remaining basil and oregano. Heat to a boil. Reduce the heat to low. Cover and cook for 15 minutes.

4. Place one third of the zucchini mixture into a blender or food processor. Cover and blend until smooth. Pour the mixture into a large bowl. Repeat the blending process twice more with the remaining zucchini mixture. Return all of the puréed mixture to the saucepan. Cook over medium heat for 5 minutes or until hot.

5. Divide the soup among 6 serving bowls and top with about 1 tablespoon of the sour cream mixture, using a spoon to swirl the cream in a decorative pattern on the soup surface.

prep time: 15 minutes • **cook time:** 30 minutes

sweet and sour brisket stew
makes 6 to 8 servings

1 jar (12 ounces) chili sauce
¼ cup beef broth
1 tablespoon plus 1½ teaspoons packed dark brown sugar
1 tablespoon plus 1½ teaspoons lemon juice
1 tablespoon Dijon mustard
¼ teaspoon paprika
½ teaspoon salt
¼ teaspoon black pepper
1 beef brisket, trimmed and cut into 1-inch pieces*
2 carrots, cut into ½ inch slices
1 onion, chopped
1 clove garlic, minced
1 tablespoon all-purpose flour
3 tablespoons water

Beef brisket has a heavy layer of fat, which some supermarkets trim off. If the meat is trimmed, buy 2½ pounds; if not, purchase 4 pounds, then trim and discard excess fat.

slow cooker directions

1. Combine chili sauce, broth, brown sugar, lemon juice, mustard, paprika, salt and pepper in slow cooker.

2. Add beef, carrots, onion and garlic; mix well. Cover; cook on LOW 8 hours.

3. *Turn slow cooker to HIGH.* Whisk 1 tablespoon flour into water in small bowl until smooth. Stir into slow cooker. Cook, uncovered, 15 minutes or until thickened.

chicken and three-pepper corn chowder

makes 4 servings

12 TYSON® Individually Frozen Boneless Skinless Chicken Tenderloins, thawed, cut into bite-size pieces
2 tablespoons butter or margarine
3 cups frozen pepper and onion stir-fry mixture
1 large clove garlic, minced
2 cups frozen corn
1 cup chicken broth
⅛ teaspoon ground red pepper
2 cups (8 ounces) shredded or diced pasteurized process cheese product
½ cup whipping cream
1 tablespoon chopped fresh cilantro
4 cilantro sprigs (optional)

1. Wash hands. In large skillet, melt butter over medium heat. Add frozen vegetables; cook and stir 5 to 7 minutes or until tender. Add garlic; stir 30 seconds. Remove vegetables and set aside.

2. Add chicken tenders, corn, broth and red pepper to skillet; bring to a boil. Reduce heat; cover and simmer 5 minutes. Over medium heat, add cheese and cream to chicken mixture. Cook and stir until cheese is melted and internal juices of chicken run clear. (Or insert instant-read meat thermometer into thickest part of chicken. Temperature should read 180°F.) Stir in chopped cilantro.

3. Ladle into individual bowls. Garnish with cilantro sprigs. Refrigerate leftovers immediately.

cook time: 25 minutes

russian borscht
makes 12 servings

    4 cups thinly sliced green cabbage
 1½ pounds beets, shredded
    5 carrots, halved lengthwise and cut into
        1-inch pieces
    1 parsnip, halved lengthwise and cut into
        1-inch pieces
    1 cup chopped onion
    4 cloves garlic, minced
    1 pound beef stew meat, cut into ½-inch cubes
    1 can (about 14 ounces) diced tomatoes
    3 cans (about 14 ounces each) reduced-sodium beef broth
 ¼ cup lemon juice
    1 tablespoon sugar
    1 teaspoon black pepper
      Sour cream (optional)
      Chopped fresh Italian parsley (optional)

slow cooker directions

1. Layer cabbage, beets, carrots, parsnip, onion, garlic, beef, tomatoes, broth, lemon juice, sugar and pepper in slow cooker. Cover; cook on LOW 7 to 9 hours.

2. Top with sour cream and sprinkle with parsley just before serving, if desired.

spring pea & mint soup
makes 6 servings

- **1 tablespoon butter**
- **1 tablespoon vegetable oil**
- **3 small leeks, white part only, cleaned and diced (about 2 cups)**
- **4 cups SWANSON® Chicken Broth (Regular, Natural Goodness® or Certified Organic)**
- **1 medium Yukon gold potato, diced (about 1 cup)**
- **1 package (16 ounces) frozen peas (3 cups)**
- **½ cup heavy cream or crème fraîche**
- **¼ cup thinly sliced fresh mint leaves**
- **1 cup PEPPERIDGE FARM® Seasoned Croutons, any variety**

1. Heat the butter and oil in a 3-quart saucepan over medium heat. Add the leeks and cook until they're tender.

2. Stir in the broth and potato. Heat to a boil. Reduce the heat to low and cook for 20 minutes or until the potato is tender.

3. Stir in the peas. Cook for 10 minutes or until the peas are tender.

4. Place one third of the broth mixture into a blender or food processor. Cover and blend until smooth. Pour the mixture into a large bowl. Repeat the blending process twice more with the remaining broth mixture. Return all of the puréed mixture to the saucepan. Add the cream and mint. Cook over medium heat until the mixture is hot. Season to taste.

5. Divide the soup among 6 serving bowls. Top each serving of soup with croutons.

prep time: 10 minutes • **cook time:** 45 minutes

spicy thai coconut soup
makes 4 servings

      2 cups chicken broth
      1 can (about 14 ounces) light coconut milk
      1 tablespoon minced fresh ginger
  ½ to 1 teaspoon red curry paste
      3 cups coarsely shredded cooked chicken (about 12 ounces)
      1 can (15 ounces) straw mushrooms, drained
      1 can (about 8 ounces) baby corn, drained
      2 tablespoons lime juice
  ¼ cup chopped fresh cilantro

1. Combine broth, coconut milk, ginger and red curry paste in large saucepan; stir until blended.

2. Add chicken, mushrooms and corn. Bring to a simmer over medium heat; cook until heated through.

3. Stir in lime juice. Sprinkle with cilantro just before serving.

note: Red curry paste can be found in jars in the Asian food section of large grocery stores. Spice levels can vary between brands. Start with ½ teaspoon, then add more as desired.

firecracker tortilla soup
makes 6 servings

- **2 tablespoons olive oil**
- **1 large onion, diced**
- **1 teaspoon POLANER® Chopped Garlic**
- **1 teaspoon ground cumin**
- **1 cup ORTEGA® Thick & Chunky Salsa**
- **1 packet (1.25 ounces) ORTEGA® Chipotle Taco Seasoning Mix**
- **6 cups chicken broth**
- **10 ORTEGA® Yellow Corn Taco Shells, divided**
- **¼ cup sour cream**

Heat oil in large pot over medium heat until hot. Add onion, garlic and cumin. Cook and stir 5 minutes or until onions are tender. Stir in salsa and seasoning mix. Add chicken broth and bring to a boil. Reduce heat to low.

Break up 8 taco shells; stir into soup. Cook over low heat 15 minutes.

Purée soup in blender or food processor in batches until smooth (or use immersion blender in pot). Return puréed soup to pot and stir to combine. Serve with additional crumbled taco shells and top with dollop of sour cream.

note: Garnish with chopped green onions, cilantro, shredded Cheddar cheese or your favorite guacamole.

prep time: 10 minutes • **start-to-finish time:** 30 minutes

egg drop soup
makes 4 servings

- 4 **cups chicken broth**
- 2 **tablespoons soy sauce**
- 1 **tablespoon dry sherry**
- 1 **tablespoon water**
- 1 **tablespoon cornstarch**
- 2 **eggs, beaten**
- 2 **green onions, diagonally sliced**
- 2 **teaspoons dark sesame oil**

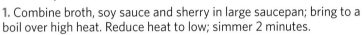

1. Combine broth, soy sauce and sherry in large saucepan; bring to a boil over high heat. Reduce heat to low; simmer 2 minutes.

2. Stir water into cornstarch in small bowl until smooth. Stir into soup until blended. Simmer 3 minutes or until slightly thickened.

3. Stirring constantly in one direction, slowly add eggs to soup in thin stream. Stir in green onions. Remove from heat; stir in sesame oil. Serve immediately.

tip: When selecting a sherry for this recipe, avoid bottles labeled "cooking sherry," which often has added salt. Choose a sherry that you would enjoy drinking.

mediterranean bean and sausage soup
makes 4 servings

- ½ **pound sweet Italian pork sausage, casing removed**
- 1 **large onion, chopped**
- ½ **teaspoon garlic powder *or* 4 cloves garlic**
- 2 **cups PREGO® Traditional Italian Sauce or PREGO® Tomato Basil & Garlic Italian Sauce**
- 1¾ **cups SWANSON® Chicken Broth (Regular, Natural Goodness® or Certified Organic)**
- 1 **can (about 15 ounces) black beans or pinto beans**
- 1 **can (about 15 ounces) white kidney beans (cannellini), drained**
- 1 **can (about 15 ounces) red kidney beans, drained**

1. Cook sausage, onion and garlic powder in saucepan over medium-high heat until sausage is browned, stirring to separate meat. Pour off fat.

2. Add sauce and broth and heat to a boil. Reduce heat to low and cook 10 minutes. Add beans and heat through.

prep time: 10 minutes • **cook time:** 25 minutes

middle eastern lamb & bean stew

makes 4 to 6 servings

    2 tablespoons olive oil
    1 lamb shank (1 to 1½ pounds)
    4 cups chicken broth
    5 cloves garlic, crushed
    8 black peppercorns
    2 slices bacon, chopped
    2 pounds lamb stew meat
    ½ cup all-purpose flour
    ½ sweet onion, chopped
    2 cans (about 15 ounces each) cannellini beans,
        rinsed and drained
    2 carrots, sliced
    2 to 3 stalks celery, sliced diagonally into 1-inch slices
    ¼ cup cornstarch
    ¼ cup water
      Salt and ground black pepper
      Chopped fresh herbs

slow cooker directions

1. Heat oil in large skillet over medium-high heat. Brown lamb shank on all sides. Place in slow cooker; add broth, garlic and peppercorns. Cover; cook on HIGH 2 hours.

2. Add bacon to skillet; cook until crisp. Drain on paper towels. Add to slow cooker. Toss stew meat with flour until coated. Working in batches, brown stew meat, adding onion to last batch. Add stew meat mixture, beans, carrots and celery to slow cooker. *Turn slow cooker to LOW.* Cover; cook 6 hours.

3. Transfer lamb shank to cutting board 30 minutes before serving. Remove meat from bone; return meat to slow cooker. Discard bone. Skim off fat from cooking liquid. Stir cornstarch into water in small bowl until smooth; stir into slow cooker. Cook, uncovered, 30 minutes or until thickened. Season with salt and ground black pepper. Garnish with chopped fresh herbs.

minestrone alla milanese
makes 8 to 10 servings

 2 cans (about 14 ounces each) reduced-sodium beef broth
 1 can (about 14 ounces) diced tomatoes
 1 cup diced potato
 1 cup coarsely chopped carrots
 1 cup coarsely chopped green cabbage
 1 cup sliced zucchini
 ¾ cup chopped onion
 ¾ cup sliced fresh green beans
 ¾ cup coarsely chopped celery
 ¾ cup water
 2 tablespoons olive oil
 1 clove garlic, minced
 ½ teaspoon dried basil
 ¼ teaspoon dried rosemary
 1 bay leaf
 1 can (about 15 ounces) cannellini beans, rinsed and drained
 Grated Parmesan cheese (optional)

slow cooker directions

1. Combine broth, tomatoes, potato, carrots, cabbage, zucchini, onion, green beans, celery, water, oil, garlic, basil, rosemary and bay leaf in slow cooker; mix well. Cover; cook on LOW 5 to 6 hours.

2. Add cannellini beans. Cover; cook 1 hour or until vegetables are tender.

3. Remove and discard bay leaf before serving. Sprinkle with Parmesan cheese, if desired.

cook time: 6 to 7 hours

wonton soup
makes 4 servings

- ¼ **pound ground pork, chicken or turkey**
- ¼ **cup finely chopped water chestnuts**
- 2 **tablespoons soy sauce, divided**
- 1 **egg white, lightly beaten**
- 1 **teaspoon minced fresh ginger**
- 12 **wonton wrappers**
- 6 **cups chicken broth**
- 1½ **cups spinach, torn**
- 1 **cup thinly sliced cooked pork (optional)**
- ½ **cup diagonally sliced green onions**
- 1 **tablespoon dark sesame oil**
- **Shredded carrot (optional)**

1. For wonton filling, combine ground pork, water chestnuts, 1 tablespoon soy sauce, egg white and ginger in small bowl; mix well.

2. Place 1 wonton wrapper with point toward edge of work surface. Mound 1 teaspoon filling near bottom point. Fold bottom point over filling, then roll wrapper over once. Moisten points with water. Bring side points together below the filling, overlapping slightly; press together firmly to seal. Repeat with remaining wrappers and filling.* Keep finished wontons covered with plastic wrap while filling remaining wrappers.

3. Combine broth and remaining 1 tablespoon soy sauce in large saucepan. Bring to a boil over high heat. Reduce heat to medium; add wontons. Simmer 4 minutes or until filling is cooked through.

4. Stir in spinach, sliced pork, if desired, and green onions. Remove from heat; stir in sesame oil. Ladle into soup bowls. Garnish with shredded carrot.

*Wontons may be made ahead to this point; cover and refrigerate up to 8 hours or freeze up to 3 months. Proceed as directed above if using refrigerated wontons; increase simmering time to 6 minutes if using frozen wontons.

creamy tuscan bean & chicken soup
makes 4 servings

2 cans (10¾ ounces each) CAMPBELL'S® Condensed Cream of Celery Soup (Regular or 98% Fat Free)

2 cups water

1 can (about 15 ounces) white kidney beans (cannellini), rinsed and drained

1 can (about 14½ ounces) diced tomatoes, undrained

2 cups shredded or diced cooked chicken

¼ cup bacon bits

3 ounces fresh baby spinach leaves (about 3 cups)

Olive oil

Grated Parmesan cheese

1. Heat the soup, water, beans, tomatoes, chicken and bacon in a 3-quart saucepan over medium-high heat to a boil.

2. Stir in the spinach. Cook for 5 minutes or until the spinach is wilted. Serve the soup with a drizzle of oil and sprinkle with the cheese.

kitchen tip: For the shredded chicken, purchase a rotisserie chicken. Remove the skin and bones. You can either shred the chicken with your fingers or use two forks.

prep time: 10 minutes • **cook time:** 10 minutes

vietnamese beef soup
makes 6 servings

  ³/₄ **pound boneless beef top sirloin or top
     round steak**
  6 **cups beef broth**
  3 **cups water**
  2 **tablespoons reduced-sodium soy sauce**
  2 **tablespoons minced fresh ginger**
  1 **cinnamon stick (3 inches long)**
  4 **ounces rice noodles (rice sticks)**
 ½ **cup thinly sliced carrots**
  2 **cups fresh bean sprouts**
  1 **red onion, halved and thinly sliced**
 ½ **cup chopped fresh cilantro**
 ½ **cup chopped fresh basil**
  2 **minced jalapeño peppers*** *or* **1 to 3 teaspoons chili sauce**

**Jalapeño peppers can sting and irritate the skin, so wear rubber gloves when handling
peppers and do not touch your eyes.*

1. Place beef in freezer 45 minutes or until firm.

2. Combine broth, water, soy sauce, ginger and cinnamon stick in
large saucepan. Bring to a boil over high heat. Reduce heat to low;
cover and simmer 20 minutes. Remove and discard cinnamon stick.

3. Place rice noodles in large bowl and cover with warm water. Let
stand 20 minutes or until softened.

4. Slice beef lengthwise in half, then crosswise into very thin strips.
Drain noodles. Place noodles and carrots in simmering broth; cook
2 to 3 minutes or until carrots are tender. Add beef and bean sprouts;
cook 1 minute or until beef is no longer pink.

5. Remove from heat; stir in onion, cilantro, basil and jalapeño peppers.
To serve, lift noodles from soup with fork and place in bowls. Ladle
remaining ingredients and broth over noodles.

italian escarole and white bean stew

makes 4 servings

    1 tablespoon olive oil
    1 onion, chopped
    3 carrots, cut into ½-inch-thick rounds
    2 cloves garlic, minced
    1 can (about 14 ounces) vegetable broth
    1 head (about 12 ounces) escarole
  ¼ teaspoon red pepper flakes
    2 cans (about 15 ounces each) Great Northern beans,
        rinsed and drained
      Salt and black pepper
      Grated Parmesan cheese (optional)

slow cooker directions

1. Heat oil in medium skillet over medium-high heat. Add onion and carrots; cook until onion is softened, stirring occasionally. Add garlic; cook and stir 1 minute. Transfer to slow cooker. Pour in broth.

2. Trim base of escarole. Roughly cut crosswise into 1-inch wide strips. Wash well in large bowl of cold water. Lift out by handfuls, leaving sand or dirt in bottom of bowl. Shake to remove excess water, but do not dry. Add to slow cooker. Sprinkle with red pepper flakes. Top with beans.

3. Cover; cook on LOW 7 to 8 hours or on HIGH 3½ to 4 hours. Season with salt and black pepper. Sprinkle with Parmesan cheese, if desired.

note: Escarole is very leafy and easily fills a slow cooker when raw, but it shrinks dramatically as it cooks down. This recipe makes four servings but can easily be doubled. Simply double the quantities of all the ingredients listed and be sure to use a large slow cooker.

green chile chicken soup with tortilla dumplings

makes 4 to 6 servings

  8 ORTEGA® Taco Shells, broken
½ cup water
⅓ cup milk
  2 onions, diced, divided
  1 egg
½ teaspoon POLANER® Minced Garlic
  1 tablespoon olive oil
  4 cups reduced-sodium chicken broth
  2 cups shredded cooked chicken
  2 tablespoons ORTEGA® Fire-Roasted Diced Green Chiles
¼ cup vegetable oil

Place taco shells, water, milk, 1 diced onion, egg and garlic in blender or food processor. Pulse several times to crush taco shells and blend ingredients. Pour into medium bowl; let stand 10 minutes to thicken.

Heat 1 tablespoon olive oil in saucepan over medium heat. Add remaining diced onion; cook and stir 4 minutes or until translucent. Stir in broth, chicken and chiles. Reduce heat to a simmer.

Heat ¼ cup vegetable oil in small skillet over medium heat. Form taco shell mixture into 1-inch balls. Drop into hot oil in batches. Cook dumplings about 3 minutes or until browned. Turn over and continue cooking 3 minutes longer or until browned. Remove dumplings; drain on paper towels. Add dumplings to soup just before serving.

note: For even more flavor, garnish the soup with chopped fresh cilantro and a squirt of lime juice.

prep time: 15 minutes • **start-to-finish time:** 30 minutes

jamaican black bean stew
makes 8 servings

        2 cups uncooked brown rice
        2 pounds sweet potatoes
        3 pounds butternut squash
        1 can (about 14 ounces) vegetable broth
        1 onion, coarsely chopped
        3 cloves garlic, minced
        1 tablespoon curry powder
    1½ teaspoons ground allspice
      ½ teaspoon ground red pepper
      ¼ teaspoon salt
        2 cans (about 15 ounces each) black beans, rinsed and drained
      ½ cup raisins
        3 tablespoons fresh lime juice
        1 cup diced tomato
        1 cup diced peeled cucumber

1. Prepare rice according to package directions.

2. Peel sweet potatoes; cut into ¾-inch chunks to measure 4 cups. Peel squash; remove seeds. Cut into ¾-inch cubes to measure 5 cups.

3. Combine sweet potatoes, squash, broth, onion, garlic, curry powder, allspice, red pepper and salt in Dutch oven. Bring to a boil over high heat. Reduce heat to low; cover and simmer 15 minutes or until sweet potatoes and squash are tender.

4. Add beans and raisins; simmer 5 minutes or until heated through. Stir in lime juice. Serve stew over rice. Top with tomato and cucumber.

chicken soup au pistou

makes 8 servings

      Olive oil cooking spray
½ **pound boneless skinless chicken breasts,**
      cut into ½-inch pieces
 1 **onion, diced**
 3 **cans (about 14 ounces each) chicken**
      broth
 1 **can (about 15 ounces) Great Northern**
      beans, rinsed and drained
 1 **can (about 14 ounces) whole tomatoes, undrained**
 2 **carrots, sliced**
 1 **large potato, diced**
¼ **teaspoon salt**
¼ **teaspoon black pepper**
 1 **cup fresh or frozen green beans, cut into 1-inch pieces**
¼ **cup pesto**
      Grated Parmesan cheese (optional)

1. Spray large saucepan with cooking spray; heat over medium-high heat. Add chicken; cook and stir 5 minutes or until browned. Add onion; cook and stir 2 minutes.

2. Add broth, Great Northern beans, tomatoes, carrots, potato, salt and pepper. Bring to a boil, stirring to break up tomatoes. Reduce heat to low; cover and simmer 15 minutes, stirring occasionally. Add green beans; cook 5 minutes or until tender.

3. Ladle soup into bowls. Top each serving with pesto and sprinkle with Parmesan cheese, if desired.

brazilian black bean soup

makes 4 to 6 servings

- **1 red onion, chopped**
- **2 cloves garlic, minced**
- **1 can (29 ounces) black beans, drained**
- **1 can (14½ ounces) vegetable or chicken broth**
- **3 tablespoons FRANK'S® REDHOT® Original Cayenne Pepper Sauce**
- **2 tablespoons chopped cilantro**
- **2 teaspoons ground cumin**
- **2 tablespoons rum or sherry (optional)**

1. Heat 1 tablespoon oil in 3-quart saucepot. Cook and stir onion and garlic 3 minutes or just until tender. Stir in 1½ cups water and remaining ingredients except rum. Heat to boiling. Reduce heat to medium-low. Cook, partially covered, 20 minutes or until flavors are blended, stirring occasionally.

2. Ladle about half of soup into blender or food processor. Cover securely. Process on low speed until mixture is smooth. Return to saucepot. Stir in rum. Cook over medium-low heat 3 minutes or until heated through and flavors are blended. Garnish with lime slices, sour cream, minced onion or cilantro, if desired.

prep time: 10 minutes • **cook time:** 30 minutes

hot and sour soup

makes 4 servings

1 package (1 ounce) dried shiitake mushrooms
4 ounces firm tofu, drained
4 cups chicken broth
3 tablespoons white vinegar
2 tablespoons soy sauce
½ to 1 teaspoon hot chili oil
¼ teaspoon white pepper
1 cup shredded cooked pork, chicken or turkey
½ cup drained canned bamboo shoots, cut into thin strips
2 tablespoons cornstarch
3 tablespoons water
1 egg white, lightly beaten
¼ cup thinly sliced green onions or chopped fresh cilantro
1 teaspoon dark sesame oil

1. Place mushrooms in small bowl; cover with warm water. Soak 20 minutes to soften. Drain; squeeze out excess water. Discard stems; slice caps. Press tofu lightly between paper towels; cut into ½-inch squares or triangles.

2. Combine broth, vinegar, soy sauce, chili oil and white pepper in medium saucepan. Bring to a boil over high heat. Reduce heat to low; simmer 2 minutes.

3. Stir in mushrooms, tofu, pork and bamboo shoots; cook and stir until heated through.

4. Stir cornstarch into water in small bowl until smooth. Stir into soup until blended. Cook and stir 4 minutes or until soup boils and thickens. Remove from heat.

5. Stirring constantly in one direction, slowly pour egg white in thin stream into soup. Stir in green onions and sesame oil.

thai roasted squash soup
makes 6 servings

- **2 tablespoons vegetable oil**
- **2 teaspoons curry powder**
- **1 butternut squash, peeled, seeded and cut into 2-inch pieces (about 6 cups)**
- **1 large sweet onion, cut into eighths**
- **1 tablespoon chopped fresh ginger root**
- **3 cups SWANSON® Chicken Broth (Regular, Natural Goodness® or Certified Organic)**
- **1 can (15 ounces) cream of coconut**
- **3 tablespoons chopped fresh cilantro leaves**

1. Heat the oven to 425°F.

2. Stir the oil and curry in a large bowl. Add the squash and onion and toss to coat. Spread the vegetables onto a 17×11-inch roasting pan.

3. Bake for 25 minutes until the vegetables are golden brown, stirring occasionally.

4. Heat the vegetables, ginger root, broth and cream of coconut in a 4-quart saucepan over medium-high heat to a boil. Reduce the heat to low. Cook for 20 minutes or until the vegetables are tender.

5. Spoon one third of the vegetable mixture into a blender or food processor. Cover and blend until smooth. Pour the mixture into a large bowl. Repeat the blending process twice more with the remaining vegetable mixture. Return all of the puréed mixture to the saucepan. Cook over medium heat until the mixture is hot. Season to taste. Divide the soup among 6 serving bowls. Sprinkle with the cilantro.

prep time: 35 minutes • **cook time:** 50 minutes

hearty chicken chili
makes 6 servings

> 1 onion, finely chopped
> 1 jalapeño pepper,* minced
> 1 clove garlic, minced
> 1½ teaspoons chili powder
> ¾ teaspoon salt
> ½ teaspoon ground cumin
> ½ teaspoon dried oregano
> ½ teaspoon black pepper
> ¼ teaspoon red pepper flakes (optional)
> 1½ pounds boneless skinless chicken thighs, cut into 1-inch pieces
> 2 cans (about 15 ounces each) hominy, rinsed and drained
> 1 can (about 15 ounces) pinto beans, rinsed and drained
> 1 cup chicken broth
> 1 tablespoon all-purpose flour
> Chopped fresh cilantro or Italian parsley (optional)

Jalapeño peppers can sting and irritate the skin, so wear rubber gloves when handling peppers and do not touch your eyes.

slow cooker directions

1. Combine onion, jalapeño pepper, garlic, chili powder, salt, cumin, oregano, black pepper and red pepper flakes, if desired, in slow cooker.

2. Add chicken, hominy, beans and broth; stir well to combine. Cover; cook on LOW 7 hours.

3. For thicker chili, stir 1 tablespoon flour into 3 tablespoons cooking liquid in small bowl until smooth. Stir into slow cooker. *Turn slow cooker to HIGH.* Cover; cook 10 minutes or until thickened. Garnish with cilantro.

chili verde
makes 4 servings

Nonstick cooking spray
¾ pound boneless lean pork, cut into
    1-inch cubes
1 pound tomatillos, husks removed, rinsed
    and coarsely chopped
1 can (about 15 ounces) Great Northern
    beans, rinsed and drained
1 can (about 14 ounces) chicken broth
1 onion, halved and thinly sliced
1 can (4 ounces) diced mild green chiles, undrained
6 cloves garlic, chopped or sliced
1 teaspoon ground cumin
    Salt and black pepper
½ cup lightly packed fresh cilantro, chopped
    Sour cream (optional)

slow cooker directions

1. Spray large skillet with cooking spray; heat over medium-high heat. Add pork; cook until browned on all sides. Transfer to slow cooker.

2. Add tomatillos, beans, broth, onion, chiles, garlic, cumin, salt and pepper. Cover; cook on HIGH 3 to 4 hours or until pork is fork-tender.

3. *Turn slow cooker to LOW.* Stir in cilantro and cook 10 minutes. Season with salt and pepper. Serve with sour cream, if desired.

easy slow-cooked chili
makes 8 servings

- 2 pounds lean ground beef
- 2 tablespoons chili powder
- 1 tablespoon ground cumin
- 1 can (28 ounces) crushed tomatoes in purée, undrained
- 1 can (15 ounces) red kidney beans, drained and rinsed
- 1 cup water
- 2 cups FRENCH'S® French Fried Onions, divided
- ¼ cup FRANK'S® REDHOT® Original Cayenne Pepper Sauce
  Sour cream and shredded Cheddar cheese

slow cooker directions

1. Cook ground beef, chili powder and cumin in large nonstick skillet over medium heat until browned, stirring frequently; drain. Transfer to slow cooker.

2. Stir in tomatoes with juice, beans, water, ½ cup French Fried Onions and FRANK'S® REDHOT® Sauce.

3. Cover; cook on LOW for 6 hours or on HIGH for 3 hours. Serve chili topped with sour cream, cheese and remaining onions.

variation: For added Cheddar flavor, substitute FRENCH'S® Cheddar French Fried Onions for the original flavor.

prep time: 10 minutes • **cook time:** 6 hours (LOW) or 3 hours (HIGH)

durango chili
makes 6 servings

3 tablespoons vegetable oil, divided
1 pound ground beef
1 pound boneless beef top sirloin steak, cut into ½-inch cubes
2 onions, chopped
1 green bell pepper, chopped
4 cloves garlic, minced
2 cans (about 14 ounces each) diced tomatoes
1 can (10¾ ounces) condensed beef broth plus 1 can water
1 bottle (12 ounces) beer
2 cans (4 ounces each) diced green chiles, undrained
3 to 5 jalapeño peppers,* minced
5 tablespoons chili powder
¼ cup tomato paste
2 bay leaves
1 teaspoon *each* salt and ground cumin
½ teaspoon black pepper
2 cans (about 15 ounces each) pinto or kidney beans,
    rinsed and drained
Shredded Cheddar cheese and sliced green onions

*Jalapeño peppers can sting and irritate the skin, so wear rubber gloves when handling peppers and do not touch your eyes.

1. Heat 1 tablespoon oil in Dutch oven over medium-high heat. Brown ground beef, stirring to break up meat. Add cubed beef; cook until browned, stirring occasionally. Transfer to plate.

2. Heat remaining 2 tablespoons oil in Dutch oven over medium heat. Add onions, bell pepper and garlic; cook and stir until tender. Return meat to Dutch oven. Stir in tomatoes, broth, water, beer, chiles, jalapeño peppers, chili powder, tomato paste, bay leaves, salt, cumin and black pepper.

3. Bring to a boil over high heat. Reduce heat to low; simmer, partially covered, 2 hours or until meat is very tender. Stir in beans. Simmer, uncovered, until heated through. Remove and discard bay leaves before serving. Top with cheese and green onions.

fireball vegetarian chili
makes 6 servings

- **1 onion, chopped**
- **2 cloves garlic, minced**
- **2 cans (15 to 19 ounces each) red kidney beans, rinsed and drained**
- **1½ cups coarsely chopped zucchini**
- **1½ cups coarsely chopped carrots**
- **1 can (15 ounces) crushed tomatoes in purée, undrained**
- **1 can (7 ounces) whole kernel corn, drained**
- **1 can (4½ ounces) chopped green chilies, drained**
- **¼ cup FRANK'S® REDHOT® Original Cayenne Pepper Sauce**
- **1 tablespoon ground cumin**

1. Heat 1 tablespoon oil in large saucepot. Cook and stir onion and garlic 3 minutes or just until tender. Add remaining ingredients; stir until well blended.

2. Heat to boiling. Reduce heat to medium-low. Cook, partially covered, 20 minutes or until vegetables are tender and flavors are blended. Serve with hot cooked rice.

prep time: 15 minutes • **cook time:** 25 minutes

cowboy coffee chili
makes 6 servings

3 pounds boneless pork shoulder, trimmed and cut into 1½-inch pieces
2 tablespoons all-purpose flour
2 tablespoons vegetable oil
1 onion, chopped
3 cloves garlic, minced
3½ cups enchilada sauce
2 cups strong brewed coffee
2 cans (about 15 ounces each) chili beans
2 cans (about 15 ounces each) pinto beans, rinsed and drained
Sliced green onions, shredded Cheddar cheese and sour cream (optional)

1. Place pork and flour in large resealable food storage bag; shake to coat.

2. Heat oil in Dutch oven over medium-high heat. Working in batches, brown pork on all sides. Transfer to plate.

3. Add onion to Dutch oven; cook and stir until golden. Add garlic; cook and stir 30 seconds.

4. Return pork and accumulated juices to Dutch oven. Stir in enchilada sauce and coffee. Reduce heat to low; simmer 2 hours or until pork is tender.

5. Stir in chili beans and pinto beans; simmer 10 minutes. Serve with green onions, Cheddar cheese and sour cream, if desired.

black bean, corn and turkey chili
makes 6 servings

- 1 tablespoon vegetable oil
- 1 pound ground turkey
- 1 large onion, chopped (about 1 cup)
- 2 tablespoons chili powder
- 1 teaspoon ground cumin
- 1 teaspoon dried oregano leaves, crushed
- ½ teaspoon ground black pepper
- ¼ teaspoon garlic powder *or* 2 cloves garlic, minced
- 1¾ cups SWANSON® Chicken Stock
- 1 cup PACE® Picante Sauce
- 1 tablespoon sugar
- 1 can (about 15 ounces) black beans, rinsed and drained
- 1 can (about 16 ounces) whole kernel corn, drained

1. Heat the oil in a 4-quart saucepan over medium-high heat. Add the turkey, onion, chili powder, cumin, oregano, black pepper and garlic powder. Cook until the turkey is well browned, stirring often to separate meat.

2. Stir the stock, picante sauce, sugar, beans and corn in the saucepan and heat to a boil. Reduce the heat to low. Cover and cook for 30 minutes or until the mixture is hot and bubbling.

prep time: 15 minutes • **cook time:** 40 minutes

beef and black bean chili
makes 4 servings

- 1 tablespoon vegetable oil
- 1 pound boneless beef round steak, cut into 1-inch cubes
- 1 can (about 15 ounces) black beans, rinsed and drained
- 1 can (about 14 ounces) fire roasted diced tomatoes
- 1 package (14 ounces) frozen bell pepper and onion mixture
- 2 tablespoons chili powder
- 1 tablespoon minced garlic
- 2 teaspoons ground cumin
- ½ ounce semisweet chocolate, chopped
- 2 cups hot cooked white rice
  Shredded Cheddar cheese (optional)

slow cooker directions

1. Heat oil in large skillet over medium-high heat. Add beef; cook 5 minutes or until browned on all sides, turning occasionally. Transfer to slow cooker.

2. Stir in beans, tomatoes, bell pepper and onion mixture, chili powder, garlic and cumin. Cover; cook on LOW 8 to 9 hours. Turn off heat and stir in chocolate until melted.

3. Serve over rice and garnish with Cheddar cheese.

pumpkin chili mexicana
makes 6 to 8 servings

   2 tablespoons vegetable oil
 ½ cup chopped onion
   1 cup chopped red or green bell pepper
   1 clove garlic, finely chopped
   1 pound ground turkey
   2 cans (14½ ounces each) no-salt-added
      diced tomatoes, undrained
   1 can (15 ounces) LIBBY'S® 100% Pure
      Pumpkin
   1 can (15 ounces) tomato sauce
   1 can (15¼ ounces) kidney beans, drained
   1 can (4 ounces) diced green chiles
 ½ cup loose-pack frozen whole kernel corn
   1 tablespoon chili powder
   1 teaspoon ground cumin
 ½ teaspoon ground black pepper

HEAT oil in large saucepan over medium-high heat. Add onion, bell pepper and garlic; cook, stirring frequently, for 5 to 7 minutes or until tender. Add turkey; cook until browned. Drain.

ADD tomatoes with juice, pumpkin, tomato sauce, beans, chiles, corn, chili powder, cumin and black pepper. Bring to a boil. Reduce heat to low. Cover; cook, stirring occasionally, for 30 minutes.

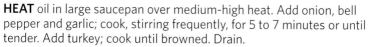

chipotle chili
makes 8 servings

    1 jar (16 ounces) PACE® Picante Sauce
    1 cup water
    2 tablespoons chili powder
    1 teaspoon ground chipotle chile pepper
    1 large onion, chopped (about 1 cup)
    2 pounds beef for stew, cut into ½-inch pieces
    1 can (about 19 ounces) red kidney beans, rinsed and drained
      Shredded Cheddar cheese (optional)
      Sour cream (optional)

slow cooker directions

1. Stir the picante sauce, water, chili powder, chipotle pepper, onion, beef and beans in a 3½-quart slow cooker.

2. Cover and cook on LOW for 8 to 9 hours* or until the beef is fork-tender. Serve with the cheese and sour cream, if desired.

Or on HIGH for 4 to 5 hours.

prep time: 15 minutes • **cook time:** 8 to 9 hours

tip: Ground chipotle chile pepper, also known as chipotle chili powder, is made from red jalapeño peppers that are smoked, dried and ground into a fine powder. It is a convenient way to add rich, smoky flavor and heat to all kinds of dishes and can be found with other spices in some large supermarkets, as well as in specialty and ethnic markets.

simple turkey chili
makes 8 servings

1 pound ground turkey
1 small onion, chopped
1 can (about 28 ounces) diced tomatoes,
    undrained
1 can (about 15 ounces) black beans,
    rinsed and drained
1 can (about 15 ounces) kidney beans,
    rinsed and drained
1 can (about 15 ounces) chickpeas, rinsed and drained
1 can (6 ounces) tomato sauce
1 can (4 ounces) chopped green chiles, drained
1 to 2 tablespoons chili powder

1. Cook turkey and onion in Dutch oven over medium-high heat until turkey is cooked through, stirring to break up meat. Drain fat.

2. Stir in tomatoes, beans, chickpeas, tomato sauce, chiles and chili powder. Bring to a boil over high heat. Reduce heat to low; simmer 20 minutes or until heated through, stirring occasionally.

note: This is an easily adaptable recipe. Substitute ground beef for turkey, pinto beans for kidney beans, or top with olives, cheese, sour cream or green onions for a simple garnish.

cincinnati chili
makes 8 servings

   1½ **pounds ground beef**
    2 **large onions, chopped (about 2 cups)**
   ¼ **teaspoon garlic powder** *or* **2 cloves garlic, minced**
    2 **teaspoons chili powder**
   ¼ **teaspoon ground cinnamon**
      Dash ground cloves
    4 **cups CAMPBELL'S® Tomato Juice**
    2 **cans (about 15 ounces each) kidney beans, drained**
      Hot cooked spaghetti

1. Cook beef, onions and garlic powder in saucepot over medium-high heat in 2 batches until beef is browned and onion is tender, stirring to separate meat. Remove beef and onion. Pour off fat. Return beef and onion to saucepot.

2. Stir in chili powder, cinnamon and cloves and cook 2 minutes. Stir in tomato juice. Heat to a boil. Cover and cook over low heat 30 minutes.

3. Add beans. Cover and cook 15 minutes, stirring occasionally. Serve over spaghetti.

prep time: 10 minutes • **cook time:** 1 hour

smokin' texas chili

makes 6 servings

       2 tablespoons olive oil
   1½ pounds boneless beef sirloin steak or top round steak
            (¾-inch thick), cut into ½-inch pieces
       1 medium onion, chopped (about ½ cup)
       2 cloves garlic, minced
       3 cups PACE® Picante Sauce
    ½ cup water
       1 tablespoon chili powder
       1 teaspoon ground cumin
       1 can (about 15 ounces) red kidney beans, rinsed and drained
    ¼ cup chopped fresh cilantro leaves
          Chili Toppings (see below)

1. Heat 1 tablespoon oil in a 6-quart saucepot over medium-high heat. Add the beef in 2 batches and cook until it's well browned, stirring often. Remove the beef from the saucepot.

2. Add the remaining oil and heat over medium heat. Add the onion and cook until it's tender. Add the garlic and cook for 30 seconds.

3. Add the picante sauce, water, chili powder and cumin. Heat to a boil. Return the beef to the saucepot. Stir in the beans. Reduce the heat to low. Cover and cook for 1 hour. Uncover and cook for 30 minutes or until the beef is fork-tender.

4. Sprinkle with the cilantro and Chili Toppings, if desired.

chili toppings: Chopped tomatoes, chopped onions, sour cream and/or shredded cheese.

prep time: 15 minutes • **cook time:** 2 hours

super chili for a crowd
makes 10 servings

2 large onions, chopped
1 tablespoon minced garlic
2 pounds boneless top round or sirloin
 steak, cut into ½-inch cubes
1 pound ground beef
1 can (28 ounces) crushed tomatoes in
 purée
1 can (15 to 19 ounces) red kidney beans,
 undrained
⅓ cup FRANK'S® REDHOT® Original Cayenne Pepper Sauce
2 packages (1¼ ounces each) chili seasoning mix

1. Heat 1 tablespoon oil in 5-quart saucepot or Dutch oven until hot. Sauté onions and garlic until tender; transfer to bowl.

2. Heat 3 tablespoons oil in same saucepot; cook meat in batches until well browned. Drain fat.

3. Add ¾ cup water and remaining ingredients to pot. Stir in onions and garlic. Heat to boiling, stirring. Simmer, partially covered, for 1 hour or until meat is tender, stirring often. Garnish as desired.

prep time: 15 minutes • **cook time:** 1 hour 15 minutes

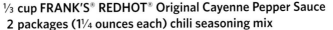

black bean vegetarian chili

makes 8 servings

1 tablespoon olive oil
2 onions, finely chopped, divided
1 green bell pepper, diced
1 teaspoon ground cumin
1 teaspoon minced garlic
4 cans (about 15 ounces each) black beans, rinsed and drained
1 can (about 15 ounces) corn, drained
1 can (about 14 ounces) diced tomatoes
1 can (6 ounces) tomato paste plus 3 cans water
1 to 2 canned chipotle peppers in adobo sauce,* drained and diced
½ teaspoon salt
½ teaspoon black pepper
Sour cream
Whole wheat flour tortillas (optional)

*Use 1 pepper for mildly spicy chili, 2 for very spicy. Freeze unused peppers and sauce in small food storage freezer bags for later use.

1. Heat oil in Dutch oven over medium-high heat. Reserve ½ cup chopped onions. Add remaining onions and bell pepper to Dutch oven; cook and stir 5 minutes or until soft. Add cumin; cook and stir 10 seconds. Add garlic; cook and stir 1 minute.

2. Stir in black beans, corn, tomatoes, tomato paste, water, chipotle peppers, salt and black pepper. Bring to a boil over high heat. Reduce heat to low; simmer 30 minutes.

3. Serve with reserved onions, sour cream and tortillas, if desired.

santa fe turkey chili
makes 6 servings

- 1 tablespoon vegetable oil
- 1 cup onion, chopped
- 2 cloves garlic, chopped
- 1 tablespoon chili powder
- 1 (16-ounce) can whole tomatoes, undrained and cut-up
- 1 (15-ounce) can herbed tomato sauce
- 1 (16-ounce) can red kidney beans, drained
- 1 cup frozen whole kernel corn
- 2 cups JENNIE-O TURKEY STORE® Turkey, cooked and cubed
- ¼ teaspoon cayenne pepper (optional)
  Yogurt, shredded cheese, sliced green onion and warm corn tortillas (optional)

In Dutch oven or large saucepan over medium-high heat, heat oil until hot. Cook onion and garlic until tender. Stir in chili powder. Add tomatoes with juice, tomato sauce, beans and corn. Reduce heat to low; cover and simmer 10 minutes, stirring occasionally. Uncover, add turkey and cayenne pepper, if desired; simmer 5 minutes. Serve with yogurt, cheese, green onion and tortillas, if desired.

prep time: 30 minutes • **cook time:** 30 minutes

chunky ancho chili with beans
makes 8 servings

5 dried ancho chiles
2 tablespoons lard or vegetable oil
1 onion, chopped
2 cloves garlic, minced
1 pound boneless beef top sirloin steak,
   cut into 1-inch cubes
1 pound boneless pork, cut into 1-inch cubes
1 to 2 jalapeño peppers,* seeded and minced
1 teaspoon salt
1 teaspoon dried oregano
1 teaspoon ground cumin
½ cup dry red wine
3 cups cooked pinto beans *or* 2 cans (about 15 ounces each)
   pinto or kidney beans, rinsed and drained

*Jalapeño peppers can sting and irritate the skin, so wear rubber gloves when handling
peppers and do not touch your eyes.*

1. Rinse ancho chiles; remove stems, seeds and veins. Place in
2-quart pan with 2 cups water. Bring to a boil; turn off heat and let
stand, covered, 30 minutes or until chiles are soft. Pour chiles with
liquid into blender or food processor; process until smooth.

2. Melt lard in Dutch oven over medium heat. Add onion and garlic;
cook and stir until onion is tender. Add beef and pork; cook, stirring
frequently, until meat is lightly browned. Add jalapeño peppers, salt,
oregano, cumin, wine and ancho purée. Bring to a boil. Cover; reduce
heat and simmer 1½ to 2 hours or until meat is very tender. Stir in
beans. Simmer, uncovered, 30 minutes or until chili has thickened
slightly.

chorizo chili
makes 6 servings

   1 pound ground beef
   8 ounces bulk raw chorizo *or* ½ package
      (15 ounces) raw chorizo
   1 can (about 16 ounces) chili beans
   2 cans (about 14 ounces each) zesty
      chili-style diced tomatoes

slow cooker directions

1. Place beef and chorizo in slow cooker. Stir to break up meat.

2. Stir in beans and tomatoes. Cover; cook on LOW 7 hours. Skim off and discard excess fat before serving.

serving suggestion: Top with sour cream or shredded cheese.

prep time: 5 minutes • **cook time:** 7 hours

> tip: The chorizo called for in this recipe is the type found in tubes in the prepared meats case, not in the deli. The deli chorizo is a hard version that is sliced much like salami.

chicken and wild rice soup
makes 4 to 6 servings

  5 cups chicken broth, divided
½ cup uncooked wild rice, rinsed and drained
¼ cup (½ stick) butter
  1 carrot, sliced
  1 onion, chopped
  2 stalks celery, chopped
½ (8-ounce) package mushrooms, sliced
  2 tablespoons all-purpose flour
¼ teaspoon salt
¼ teaspoon white pepper
1½ cups chopped cooked chicken
¼ cup dry sherry (optional)

1. Combine 2½ cups broth and rice in medium saucepan; bring to a boil. Reduce heat to medium-low; cover and simmer 1 hour or until rice is tender. Drain; set aside.

2. Melt butter in large saucepan over medium heat. Add carrot; cook and stir 3 minutes. Add onion, celery and mushrooms; cook and stir 3 to 4 minutes or until tender. Whisk in flour, salt and white pepper until smooth.

3. Gradually stir in remaining 2½ cups broth. Bring to a boil. Reduce heat to medium-low; cook and stir 2 minutes or until thickened. Stir in chicken, rice and sherry, if desired. Simmer 3 minutes or until heated through.

hearty meatball stew
makes 6 servings

     1 pound ground turkey breast or extra-lean ground beef
   ³/₄ cup QUAKER® Oats (quick or old fashioned, uncooked)
     1 can (8 ounces) no-salt-added tomato sauce, divided
  1½ teaspoons garlic powder
  1½ teaspoons dried thyme leaves, divided
     2 cans (14½ ounces each) 70% less sodium, fat-free
       chicken broth
   ³/₄ teaspoon salt (optional)
   ¹/₃ cup ditalini or other small pasta
  2½ cups any frozen vegetable blend (do not thaw)
   ¹/₄ cup water
     2 tablespoons cornstarch

1. Heat broiler. Lightly spray rack of broiler pan with nonstick cooking spray.

2. Combine turkey, oats, ¹/₃ cup tomato sauce, garlic powder and 1 teaspoon thyme in large bowl; mix lightly but thoroughly. Transfer to sheet of aluminum foil or waxed paper. Pat mixture into 9×6-inch rectangle. Cut into 1½-inch squares; roll each square into a ball. Arrange meatballs on broiler pan.

3. Broil meatballs 6 to 8 inches from heat about 6 minutes or until cooked through, turning once.

4. While meatballs cook, bring broth, remaining tomato sauce, remaining ½ teaspoon thyme and salt, if desired, to a boil in 4-quart saucepan or Dutch oven over medium-high heat. Add pasta and vegetables; return to a boil. Reduce heat, cover and simmer 10 minutes or until pasta and vegetables are tender. Stir together water and cornstarch in small bowl until smooth. Add to pan along with meatballs. Cook and stir until broth is thickened. Spoon into bowls.

ham and barley cream soup
makes 8 servings

- ¼ cup butter or margarine
- ¼ cup finely chopped onion
- 1 cup quick-cooking barley
- 5½ cups water
- 5½ teaspoons HERB-OX® chicken flavored bouillon
- 1 cup (6 ounces) HORMEL® CURE 81® ham, cut into thin slivers
- ¼ teaspoon poultry seasoning
- ¼ teaspoon white pepper
- 1 cup heavy cream
- 1 cup frozen peas, thawed
- 1 cup shredded Parmesan cheese
- Ground nutmeg

In large saucepan over medium heat, melt butter. Add onion and cook 3 to 5 minutes or until tender. Add barley; cook, stirring until light golden in color.

Stir in water, bouillon, ham, poultry seasoning and white pepper. Bring mixture to a boil; reduce heat, cover and simmer 15 minutes or until barley is tender.

Stir in cream and peas. Heat thoroughly. Top individual servings with cheese and generous sprinkle of nutmeg.

ravioli minestrone
makes 8 servings

1 package (about 9 ounces) refrigerated cheese ravioli
2 teaspoons olive oil
2 carrots, chopped
1 onion, chopped
1 stalk celery, chopped
2 cloves garlic, minced
6 cups water
1 can (about 15 ounces) chickpeas, rinsed and drained
1 can (about 14 ounces) diced tomatoes
3 tablespoons tomato paste
1 teaspoon dried basil
1 teaspoon dried oregano
¾ teaspoon salt
¾ teaspoon black pepper
2 zucchini, cut in half lengthwise and sliced
1 package (10 ounces) baby spinach

1. Cook ravioli according to package directions. Drain; keep warm.

2. Meanwhile, heat oil in Dutch oven over medium-high heat. Add carrots, onion, celery and garlic; cook 5 minutes or until vegetables are tender, stirring occasionally.

3. Stir in water, chickpeas, tomatoes, tomato paste, basil, oregano, salt and pepper. Bring to a boil over high heat.

4. Reduce heat to low; simmer 15 minutes. Add zucchini; simmer 5 minutes. Stir in spinach; simmer just until wilted. Stir in ravioli.

prep time: 20 minutes • **cook time:** 30 minutes

lentil stew over couscous
makes 12 servings

3 cups dried lentils (1 pound), sorted and rinsed
3 cups water
1 can (about 14 ounces) vegetable broth
1 can (about 14 ounces) diced tomatoes
1 onion, chopped
1 green bell pepper, chopped
4 stalks celery, chopped
1 carrot, halved lengthwise and sliced
2 cloves garlic, chopped
1 teaspoon dried marjoram
¼ teaspoon black pepper
1 tablespoon olive oil
1 tablespoon cider vinegar
4½ to 5 cups hot cooked couscous

slow cooker directions

1. Combine lentils, water, broth, tomatoes, onion, bell pepper, celery, carrot, garlic, marjoram and black pepper in slow cooker; stir well.

2. Cover; cook on LOW 8 to 9 hours.

3. Stir in oil and vinegar. Serve over couscous.

note: Lentil stew keeps well in the refrigerator for up to 1 week. It can also be frozen in an airtight container for up to three months.

prep time: 10 minutes • **cook time:** 8 to 9 hours

turkey vegetable chili mac
makes 6 servings

> Nonstick cooking spray
> ¾ pound ground turkey
> 1 can (about 15 ounces) black beans, rinsed and drained
> 1 can (about 14 ounces) Mexican-style diced tomatoes
> 1 can (about 14 ounces) diced tomatoes
> 1 cup frozen corn
> ½ cup chopped onion
> 2 cloves garlic, minced
> 1 teaspoon Mexican seasoning
> ½ cup uncooked elbow macaroni
> ⅓ cup sour cream

slow cooker directions

1. Lightly coat large nonstick skillet with cooking spray; heat over medium-high heat. Add turkey; cook and stir 5 minutes or until no longer pink. Transfer to slow cooker.

2. Add beans, tomatoes, corn, onion, garlic and seasoning. Cover; cook on LOW 4 to 5 hours.

3. Stir in macaroni. Cover; cook 30 minutes or until tender, stirring occasionally. Serve with sour cream.

savory barley & tomato soup
makes 6 servings

    1 can (10³/₄ ounces) CAMPBELL'S®
       Condensed Golden Mushroom Soup
    1 can (10¹/₂ ounces) CAMPBELL'S®
       Condensed Chicken Broth
    1 can (about 28 ounces) diced tomatoes
    2 soup cans water
    2 large onions, diced (about 2 cups)
    2 cloves garlic, minced
    3 large carrots, diced (about 1¹/₂ cups)
  ¹/₂ cup uncooked pearl barley
    1 teaspoon Italian seasoning
    2 tablespoons chopped fresh parsley
    1 cup grated Parmesan cheese
       Croutons (optional)

slow cooker directions

1. Stir soup, broth, tomatoes, water, onions, garlic, carrots, barley and Italian seasoning in a 6-quart slow cooker.

2. Cover and cook on LOW for 6 to 7 hours* or until the barley is tender, stirring once during cooking. Stir in the parsley and Parmesan cheese. Top with the croutons and additional cheese, if desired.

Or on HIGH for 4 to 5 hours.

kitchen tip: Stir in some SWANSON® Chicken Broth or water to adjust the consistency, if desired.

prep time: 15 minutes • **cook time:** 6 to 7 hours

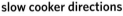

country noodle soup
makes 6 servings

  1 tablespoon I CAN'T BELIEVE IT'S NOT BUTTER!® Spread
  ¾ cup finely chopped onion
  ½ cup finely chopped red bell pepper
2½ cups water
  4 cups chicken broth or bouillon
  1 package KNORR® PASTA SIDES™-Chicken Broccoli or Chicken
  ½ cup cut-up cooked chicken, turkey or ham (optional)

Melt Spread in 4-quart saucepan over medium-high heat and cook
onion and red pepper, stirring occasionally, 5 minutes or until tender.
Stir in water and chicken broth. Bring just to a boil over high heat.

Stir in KNORR® PASTA SIDES™-Chicken Broccoli. Continue boiling
over medium heat, stirring occasionally, 8 minutes or until pasta is
tender. Stir in chicken; heat through.

prep time: 10 minutes • **cook time:** 16 minutes

> tip: This is a great way to use up leftover meats from
> previously cooked whole chickens, turkeys or hams.
> You can also use precooked chicken strips found in the
> refrigerated or frozen section of the supermarket.

greek-style chicken stew
makes 6 servings

　3 pounds skinless chicken breasts
　　All-purpose flour
　　Nonstick cooking spray
　2 cups cubed peeled eggplant
　2 cups sliced mushrooms
　¾ cup coarsely chopped onion
　2 cloves garlic, minced
　1 teaspoon dried oregano
　½ teaspoon dried basil
　½ teaspoon dried thyme
　2 cups reduced-sodium chicken broth
　¼ cup dry sherry or reduced-sodium chicken broth
　¼ teaspoon salt
　¼ teaspoon black pepper
　1 can (about 14 ounces) artichoke hearts, drained
　3 cups hot cooked wide egg noodles

1. Coat chicken very lightly with flour. Generously coat Dutch oven or large nonstick skillet with cooking spray; heat over medium heat. Add chicken; cook 10 to 15 minutes or until browned on all sides. Transfer to plate.

2. Add eggplant, mushrooms, onion, garlic, oregano, basil and thyme to Dutch oven; cook and stir over medium heat 5 minutes.

3. Return chicken to Dutch oven. Stir in broth, sherry, salt and pepper; bring to a boil over high heat. Reduce heat to low; cover and simmer 1 hour or until chicken is cooked through. Add artichokes during last 20 minutes of cooking. Serve over noodles.

salmon, corn & barley chowder

makes 2 to 4 servings

1 teaspoon canola oil
¼ cup chopped onion
1 clove garlic, minced
2½ cups reduced-sodium chicken broth
¼ cup uncooked quick-cooking barley
1 can (4 ounces) salmon, drained
1 cup frozen corn, thawed
⅓ cup milk
1 tablespoon all-purpose flour
1 tablespoon water
½ teaspoon chili powder
¼ teaspoon ground cumin
¼ teaspoon dried oregano
⅛ teaspoon salt
1 tablespoon minced fresh cilantro
⅛ teaspoon black pepper
    Lime wedges (optional)

1. Heat oil in medium saucepan over medium heat. Add onion and garlic; cook and stir 1 to 2 minutes or until onion is tender.

2. Add broth; bring to a boil over high heat. Stir in barley. Reduce heat to low; cover and simmer 10 minutes or until barley is tender.

3. Remove and discard bones and skin from salmon; flake into bite-size pieces. Add salmon, corn and milk to saucepan; stir until blended.

4. Stir flour into water in small bowl until smooth. Stir into saucepan. Add chili powder, cumin, oregano and salt; stir well. Simmer 2 to 3 minutes or until slightly thickened. Stir in cilantro and pepper. Serve with lime wedges, if desired.

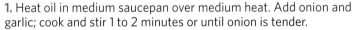

quaker's oatmeal soup
makes 4 servings

- **1 onion, finely chopped (about ¾ cup)**
- **½ cup shredded carrots**
- **3 tablespoons butter or margarine, divided**
- **½ cup QUAKER® Oats (quick or old fashioned, uncooked)**
- **6 cups chicken broth**
- **1 cup QUAKER® Oats (quick or old fashioned, cooked according to package directions)**
- **Salt and black pepper**
- **3 tablespoons finely chopped fresh parsley *or* 1 tablespoon dried parsley flakes**

1. Cook onion and carrots in 2 tablespoons butter in large skillet or saucepan over medium-low heat, stirring often, 5 minutes or until onion is tender. Add uncooked oats and remaining 1 tablespoon butter. Cook, stirring often, 3 minutes or until oats are golden brown.

2. Stir in broth; bring to a low boil. Add cooked oatmeal, stirring until well mixed. Cook over medium heat 5 minutes. Season to taste with salt and pepper. Sprinkle with parsley.

wild rice and asparagus soup

makes 2 servings

½ cup uncooked instant wild rice
½ pound thin asparagus spears
1½ teaspoons butter
1 minced shallot *or* ¼ cup minced red onion
1 tablespoon all-purpose flour
1 cup chicken broth
½ cup half-and-half
¼ teaspoon dried thyme
⅛ teaspoon black pepper

1. Cook rice according to package directions. Drain; set aside.

2. Meanwhile, trim asparagus. Place in skillet with water to cover. Cook over medium-high heat 5 minutes or until tender. Drain. Cut asparagus into 1-inch pieces.

3. Melt butter in medium saucepan over medium heat. Add shallot; cook 3 minutes or until tender, stirring occasionally. Stir in flour until absorbed. Stir in broth; cook 1 to 2 minutes or until slightly thickened. Add half-and-half, thyme and pepper. Stir in cooked rice and asparagus. Reduce heat to low; simmer 5 minutes.

note: If you prefer, you can cook regular wild rice instead of using instant. However, wild rice requires longer cooking than other rices. Avoid overcooking because it will lose its characteristic chewy texture.

hearty lasagna soup
makes 4 servings

- **1 pound ground beef**
- **1 small onion, chopped (about ¼ cup)**
- **1 teaspoon minced garlic**
- **¼ teaspoon dried parsley flakes**
- **3½ cups SWANSON® Beef Broth (Regular, 50% Less Sodium or Certified Organic)**
- **1 can (14½ ounces) diced tomatoes**
- **¼ teaspoon Italian seasoning, crushed**
- **1½ cups uncooked mafalda or corkscrew-shaped pasta**
- **¼ cup grated Parmesan cheese**

1. Cook the beef, onion, garlic and parsley in a 3-quart saucepan over medium-high heat for 10 minutes or until it's well browned, stirring often to separate the meat. Pour off any fat.

2. Stir the broth, tomatoes and Italian seasoning in the saucepan and heat to a boil.

3. Stir the pasta in the saucepan. Reduce the heat to medium and cook for 10 minutes or until the pasta is tender. Stir in the cheese. Serve with additional cheese, if desired.

prep time: 10 minutes • **cook time:** 25 minutes

greens, white bean and barley soup

makes 6 to 8 servings

2 tablespoons olive oil
3 carrots, diced
1½ cups chopped onions
2 cloves garlic, minced
1½ cups sliced mushrooms
6 cups vegetable broth
2 cups cooked pearl barley
1 can (about 15 ounces) Great Northern beans,
    rinsed and drained
2 bay leaves
1 teaspoon sugar
1 teaspoon dried thyme
7 cups chopped stemmed collard greens
1 tablespoon white wine vinegar
    Hot pepper sauce
    Red bell pepper strips (optional)

1. Heat oil in Dutch oven over medium heat. Add carrots, onions and garlic; cook and stir 3 minutes. Add mushrooms; cook and stir 5 minutes or until carrots are tender.

2. Add broth, barley, beans, bay leaves, sugar and thyme. Bring to a boil over high heat. Reduce heat to low; cover and simmer 5 minutes.

3. Add greens; simmer, uncovered, 10 minutes. Remove and discard bay leaves. Stir in vinegar. Season with hot pepper sauce. Garnish with bell peppers.

italian wedding soup
makes 6 servings

  1 tablespoon olive oil
  1 pound bulk Italian sausage*
  ½ cup chopped onion
  ½ cup chopped carrots
  1 teaspoon Italian seasoning
 7½ cups reduced-sodium chicken broth
  3 cups packed coarsely chopped kale
  **1 cup uncooked ditalini or other small
     shaped pasta**
  Grated Parmesan cheese (optional)

If bulk sausage is not available, use sausage links and remove the casings.

1. Heat oil in Dutch oven or large saucepan over medium-high heat. Add sausage, onion, carrots and seasoning; cook and stir 4 minutes or until sausage is cooked through. Drain fat.

2. Stir in broth and kale; bring to a boil over high heat. Stir in pasta. Reduce heat to low; simmer, partially covered, 9 minutes or until pasta is tender. Sprinkle with Parmesan cheese, if desired.

tip: Kale is available year-round but its flavor is best during the winter months.

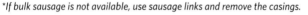

hearty vegetable pasta soup

makes 6 servings

 1 tablespoon vegetable oil
 1 onion, chopped
 3 cups chicken broth
 1 can (about 14 ounces) diced tomatoes
 1 large potato, peeled and cubed
 2 carrots, sliced
 1 stalk celery, sliced
 1 teaspoon dried basil
 $\frac{1}{2}$ teaspoon salt
 $\frac{1}{8}$ teaspoon black pepper
 $\frac{1}{3}$ cup uncooked tiny bowtie pasta
 2 ounces fresh spinach, stemmed and chopped

1. Heat oil in Dutch oven over medium-high heat. Add onion; cook and stir until translucent. Add broth, tomatoes, potato, carrots, celery, basil, salt and pepper; bring to a boil over high heat.

2. Reduce heat to low; simmer 20 minutes or until potato and carrots are tender, stirring occasionally.

3. Stir in pasta; simmer 8 minutes or until pasta is tender.

4. Stir in spinach; simmer 2 minutes or until wilted. Serve immediately.

turkey taco soup
makes 6 servings

  1 tablespoon olive oil
½ cup diced onions
  1 tablespoon POLANER® Minced Garlic
  1 pound ground turkey
  1 tablespoon ORTEGA® Chili Seasoning Mix
½ teaspoon salt
½ teaspoon black pepper
  3 cups chicken broth
  1 can (16 ounces) ORTEGA® Refried Beans
  1 tablespoon ORTEGA® Fire-Roasted Diced Green Chiles
  1 cup shredded lettuce
½ cup chopped tomato
  4 ORTEGA® Yellow Corn Taco Shells, crumbled

Heat oil in large saucepan over medium heat. Add onions and garlic; cook and stir 5 minutes. Stir in turkey, seasoning mix, salt and pepper. Cook and stir 5 minutes to break up turkey.

Add broth, beans and chiles; stir until beans are mixed in well. Cook over medium heat 10 minutes. Serve with lettuce, tomato and crumbled taco shells.

prep time: 5 minutes • **start-to-finish time:** 20 minutes

hearty 3-bean & ham soup

makes 6 to 8 servings

- **1 cup chopped onion**
- **1 tablespoon vegetable or olive oil**
- **1 (15-ounce) can *each* pinto beans, black beans and red kidney beans, drained and rinsed**
- **1 cup sliced carrots**
- **3½ cups water**
- **4 cubes HERB-OX® beef bouillon**
- **1 (14½-ounce) can diced tomatoes**
- **⅓ cup chili sauce**
- **3 tablespoons cider vinegar**
- **1 tablespoon firmly packed brown sugar**
- **2 teaspoons Worcestershire sauce**
- **2 teaspoons prepared mustard**
- **1 cup diced ham**
- **2 tablespoons chopped fresh parsley**

In large saucepan, sauté onion in oil until golden. Stir in beans and next 9 ingredients. Bring mixture to a boil.

Reduce heat, cover and simmer for 25 to 30 minutes or until carrots are tender. Stir in ham and parsley. Ladle into bowls and serve.

smoked sausage and navy bean soup

makes 8 servings

8 cups chicken broth
1 pound dried navy beans, rinsed and sorted
2 ham hocks (about 1 pound total)
2 onions, diced
1 can (about 14 ounces) diced tomatoes
1 cup diced carrots
1 cup diced celery
2 tablespoons tomato paste
2 cloves garlic, minced
1 bay leaf
1 teaspoon dried thyme
1 pound smoked sausage, cut into ½-inch rounds

slow cooker directions

1. Bring broth to a boil in large saucepan over medium-high heat. Cover; reduce heat to low.

2. Place beans in slow cooker. Add ham hocks, onions, tomatoes, carrots, celery, tomato paste, garlic, bay leaf and thyme. Carefully pour in hot broth. Cover; cook on HIGH 8 to 9 hours or until beans are tender.

3. Remove and discard bay leaf. Remove ham hocks; let stand until cool enough to handle. Remove ham from hocks; chop and return to slow cooker. Discard bones.

4. Stir in sausage. Cover; cook 15 to 30 minutes or until sausage is heated through.

black bean and bacon soup
makes 6 to 8 servings

- **5 strips bacon, sliced**
- **1 medium onion, diced**
- **2 tablespoons ORTEGA® Fire-Roasted Diced Green Chiles**
- **2 cans (15 ounces each) ORTEGA® Black Beans, undrained**
- **4 cups chicken broth**
- **½ cup ORTEGA® Taco Sauce**
- **½ cup sour cream**
- **4 ORTEGA® Yellow Corn Taco Shells, crumbled**

Cook bacon in large pot over medium heat 5 minutes or until crisp. Add onion and chiles. Cook 5 minutes or until onion begins to brown. Stir in beans, broth and taco sauce. Bring to a boil. Reduce heat to low. Simmer 20 minutes.

Purée half of soup in food processor until smooth (or use immersion blender in pot). Return puréed soup to pot and stir to combine. Serve with a dollop of sour cream and crumbled taco shells.

note: For a less chunky soup, purée the entire batch and cook an additional 15 minutes.

prep time: 5 minutes • **start-to-finish time:** 30 minutes

tip: Bacon gives this classic soup a rich smoky flavor that will delight your guests.

chickpea and squash stew

makes 2 servings

    1 teaspoon canola oil
 3/4 cup chopped onion
    1 jalapeño pepper,* seeded and minced
    1 (1/2-inch) piece fresh ginger, peeled and
        minced
    1 clove garlic, minced
    2 teaspoons ground cumin
 1/2 teaspoon ground coriander
    1 cup cubed peeled butternut squash, sweet potato or pumpkin
    1 cup canned chickpeas, rinsed and drained
 1/2 cup water
 1/2 tablespoon reduced-sodium soy sauce
    1 cup coconut milk
      Juice of 1 lime
 1/4 cup chopped fresh cilantro
      Spinach leaves (optional)

Jalapeño peppers can sting and irritate the skin, so wear rubber gloves when handling peppers and do not touch your eyes.

1. Heat oil in medium saucepan over medium-low heat. Add onion, jalapeño pepper, ginger and garlic; cook and stir 2 to 3 minutes or until onion is tender. Add cumin and coriander; cook and stir 1 minute.

2. Add squash, chickpeas, water and soy sauce to saucepan. Bring to a boil over high heat. Reduce heat to low; simmer 15 minutes or until squash is tender. Add coconut milk; cook and stir 2 minutes or until heated through. Stir in lime juice and cilantro. Garnish with spinach.

red bean soup with andouille sausage

makes 6 to 8 servings

- **2 tablespoons butter**
- **1 onion, diced**
- **3 stalks celery, diced**
- **2 cloves garlic, chopped**
- **8 cups chicken broth**
- **1½ cups dried red kidney beans, soaked in cold water 1 hour, rinsed and drained**
- **1 ham hock**
- **1 bay leaf**
- **2 parsnips, diced**
- **1 sweet potato, peeled and diced**
- **1 pound andouille sausage or kielbasa, sliced ½ inch thick**
   Salt and black pepper

slow cooker directions

1. Melt butter in large skillet over medium heat. Add onion, celery and garlic; cook and stir 5 minutes or until tender. Transfer to slow cooker.

2. Add broth, beans, ham hock and bay leaf to slow cooker. Cover; cook on HIGH 2 hours.

3. Remove ham hock; let stand until cool enough to handle. Remove ham from hock; chop and return to slow cooker. Discard bone. Add parsnips and sweet potato. Cover; cook 2 hours.

4. Add sausage. Cover; cook 30 minutes or until heated through. Remove and discard bay leaf before serving. Season with salt and pepper.

sausage and bean ragoût
makes 6 servings

- 2 tablespoons olive oil
- 1 pound ground beef
- 1 pound hot Italian pork sausage, casing removed
- 1 large onion, chopped (about 1 cup)
- 4 cloves garlic, minced
- 3½ cups SWANSON® Chicken Stock
- ¼ cup chopped fresh basil leaves
- 2 cans (14½ ounces each) Italian-style diced tomatoes
- 1 can (about 15 ounces) white kidney beans (cannellini), rinsed and drained
- ½ cup uncooked elbow pasta
- 1 bag (6 ounces) fresh baby spinach leaves
- ⅓ cup grated Romano cheese

1. Heat the oil in a 6-quart saucepot over medium-high heat. Add the beef, sausage and onion and cook until the beef and sausage are well browned, stirring often to separate meat. Pour off any fat. Add the garlic and cook and stir for 30 seconds.

2. Stir the stock, basil, tomatoes and beans in the saucepot and heat to a boil. Reduce the heat to low. Cover and cook for 10 minutes, stirring occasionally. Add the pasta and cook until it's tender.

3. Stir in the spinach and cook until wilted. Remove the saucepot from the heat and stir in the cheese. Serve with additional cheese, if desired.

kitchen tip: This recipe calls for cooking the pasta until it's tender. However, if you like your pasta a little al dente, that will work as well.

prep time: 15 minutes • **cook time:** 40 minutes

spicy four bean stew
makes 4 to 6 servings

- 2 tablespoons vegetable oil
- 1 onion, coarsely chopped
- 3 cloves garlic, chopped
- 1 zucchini, halved lengthwise and thinly sliced
- ½ red bell pepper, chopped
- 2 cans (11 ounces each) tomatillos, drained
- 1 can (about 15 ounces) red kidney beans, rinsed and drained
- 1 can (about 15 ounces) black beans, rinsed and drained
- 1 can (about 15 ounces) Great Northern beans, rinsed and drained
- 1 can (about 15 ounces) chickpeas, rinsed and drained
- 1 can (15 ounces) tomato sauce
- ½ cup barbecue sauce
- 1½ teaspoons ground cumin
- 1 to 1½ teaspoons chili powder
- ½ teaspoon salt
- ¼ to ½ teaspoon ground red pepper

Toppings: sour cream, chopped tomato, chopped onion and/or shredded Cheddar cheese (optional)

Chopped fresh cilantro (optional)

1. Heat oil in Dutch oven over medium-high heat. Add onion and garlic; cook and stir until onion is soft. Stir in zucchini and bell pepper; cook and stir 5 minutes.

2. Add tomatillos, beans, chickpeas, tomato sauce, barbecue sauce, cumin, chili powder, salt and ground red pepper. Bring to a boil over high heat. Reduce heat to low; cover and simmer 30 minutes.

3. Serve with toppings, if desired. Garnish with cilantro.

country bean soup

makes 6 servings

- 1¼ cups dried navy beans or lima beans, rinsed and sorted
- ¼ pound ham or salt pork, chopped
- ¼ cup chopped onion
- ½ teaspoon dried oregano
- ¼ teaspoon salt
- ¼ teaspoon ground ginger
- ¼ teaspoon dried sage
- ¼ teaspoon black pepper
- 2 cups milk
- 2 tablespoons butter

1. Place beans in large saucepan; cover with water. Bring to a boil over high heat. Reduce heat to low; simmer 2 minutes. Remove from heat; cover and let stand for 1 hour.

2. Drain beans and return to saucepan. Stir in 2½ cups water, ham, onion, oregano, salt, ginger, sage and pepper. Bring to a boil over high heat.

3. Reduce heat to low; cover and simmer 2 hours or until beans are tender. (If necessary, add more water to keep beans covered during cooking.) Stir in milk and butter; cook and stir until heated through.

lentil soup with beef
makes 8 servings

   3 cans (10½ ounces each) CAMPBELL'S® Condensed
      French Onion Soup
   1 soup can water
   3 stalks celery, sliced (about 1½ cups)
   3 large carrots, sliced (about 1½ cups)
1½ cups dried lentils
   1 can (about 14½ ounces) diced tomatoes
   1 teaspoon dried thyme leaves, crushed
   3 cloves garlic, minced
   2 pounds beef for stew, cut into 1-inch pieces

slow cooker directions
1. Stir the soup, water, celery, carrots, lentils, tomatoes, thyme, garlic and beef in a 5-quart slow cooker. Season as desired.

2. Cover and cook on LOW for 7 to 8 hours* or until the beef is fork-tender.

Or on HIGH for 4 to 5 hours.

prep time: 15 minutes • **cook time:** 7 to 8 hours

garden chickpea soup
makes 6 to 8 servings

- ½ pound USA dried chickpeas
- 2 tablespoons olive oil
- 1 medium onion, diced
- 2 cloves garlic, minced
- ½ teaspoon dried oregano
- ½ teaspoon dried thyme
- ¼ teaspoon black pepper
- 2 medium carrots, diced
- 2 stalks celery, diced
- 5 cups reduced-sodium chicken broth
- 4 cups water
- 2 medium potatoes, peeled and diced
- 2 medium parsnips, peeled and diced
- ½ cup broccoli florets
- 1 ounce sun-dried tomatoes, diced

Soak the chickpeas overnight in cold water. When ready to cook the soup, drain the chickpeas and set aside. Heat the olive oil in a stockpot over medium-low heat. Add the onion, garlic, oregano, thyme and pepper. Sauté the mixture, stirring occasionally, until the onions are translucent, 8 to 10 minutes. Add the carrots and celery and sauté for another 3 to 4 minutes. Add the broth, chickpeas and 4 cups water; bring to a boil. Reduce the heat and simmer for 1 hour. Add the potatoes and parsnips; simmer for another 15 minutes. Add the broccoli and sun-dried tomatoes. Simmer 10 minutes longer. Serve hot.

Favorite recipe from **USA Dry Pea & Lentil Council**

black bean and turkey stew

makes 6 servings

   3 cans (about 15 ounces each) black
        beans, rinsed and drained
1½ cups chopped onions
1½ cups reduced-sodium chicken broth
   1 cup sliced celery
   1 cup chopped red bell pepper
   4 cloves garlic, minced
1½ teaspoons dried oregano
 ¾ teaspoon ground coriander
 ½ teaspoon ground cumin
 ¼ teaspoon ground red pepper
   6 ounces cooked turkey sausage, thinly sliced

slow cooker directions

1. Combine beans, onions, broth, celery, bell pepper, garlic, oregano, coriander, cumin and ground red pepper. Cover; cook on LOW 6 to 8 hours.

2. Transfer about 1½ cups bean mixture to blender or food processor; process until smooth. Return to slow cooker. Stir in sausage. Cover; cook on LOW 10 to 15 minutes or until heated through.

southwestern chicken & white bean soup

makes 6 servings

1 tablespoon vegetable oil
1 pound skinless, boneless chicken breast, cut into 1-inch pieces
1¾ cups SWANSON® Chicken Broth (Regular, Natural Goodness® or Certified Organic)
1 cup PACE® Picante Sauce
3 cloves garlic, minced
2 teaspoons ground cumin
1 can (about 16 ounces) small white beans, rinsed and drained
1 cup frozen whole kernel corn
1 large onion, chopped (about 1 cup)

slow cooker directions

1. Heat the oil in a 10-inch skillet over medium-high heat. Add the chicken and cook until it's well browned, stirring often.

2. Stir the chicken, broth, picante sauce, garlic, cumin, beans, corn and onion in a 3½-quart slow cooker.

3. Cover and cook on LOW for 8 to 9 hours* or until the chicken is cooked through.

Or on HIGH for 4 to 5 hours.

prep time: 15 minutes • **cook time:** 8 to 9 hours

rich red bean soup
makes 6 servings

1 pound dried red kidney beans
2 tablespoons butter
1 onion, finely chopped
4 carrots, chopped
2 stalks celery, chopped
1 pound smoked ham hocks
3 cloves garlic, finely chopped
1 bay leaf
1 sprig thyme
1 sprig parsley
½ teaspoon salt
¼ teaspoon black pepper
2 tablespoons fresh lemon juice
Sour cream (optional)

1. Soak beans in water in large bowl 6 hours or overnight. Drain, rinse and set aside.

2. Melt butter in Dutch oven over medium-high heat. Add onion; cook and stir 3 minutes or until softened. Add carrots and celery; cook and stir 5 minutes or until browned.

3. Add 1½ quarts water, beans, ham hocks, garlic, bay leaf, thyme and parsley. Bring to a boil over high heat. Reduce heat to low; cover and simmer 1 hour 30 minutes or until beans are softened.

4. Remove ham hocks; let stand until cool enough to handle. Remove ham from hocks; chop and return to slow cooker. Discard bones, bay leaf, thyme and parsley. Stir in salt and pepper.

5. Process soup in batches in food processor or blender until smooth. Return to Dutch oven. Bring to a simmer; stir in lemon juice. Garnish with sour cream.

spiced carrot, lentil and coriander soup

makes 6 to 8 servings

    3 tablespoons **FILIPPO BERIO**® Olive Oil
    1 large onion, sliced
    1 pound carrots, sliced
    8 ounces dried red or brown lentils (about 1¼ cups),
        rinsed and drained
    2 teaspoons ground coriander
    2 teaspoons ground cumin
    6 cups chicken broth
    2 cups milk
       Salt and freshly ground black pepper
       Fresh cilantro sprigs (optional)

In large saucepan, heat olive oil over medium heat until hot. Add onion and carrots; cook and stir 5 minutes. Add lentils, coriander and cumin; cook and stir 1 minute. Stir in chicken broth; bring to a boil. Cover; reduce heat to low and simmer 30 minutes or until lentils and carrots are tender. Cool slightly.

Process soup in small batches in food processor or blender container until smooth. Return soup to saucepan; stir in milk. Heat through. Season to taste with salt and pepper. Garnish with cilantro, if desired. Serve hot.

hearty lentil and root vegetable stew
makes 8 servings

       2 cans (about 14 ounces each) chicken broth
   1½ cups diced turnip
       1 cup dried red lentils, rinsed and sorted
       1 onion, cut into ½-inch wedges
       2 carrots, cut into 1-inch pieces
       1 red bell pepper, cut into 1-inch pieces
    ½ teaspoon dried oregano
    ⅛ teaspoon red pepper flakes
       1 tablespoon olive oil
    ½ teaspoon salt
       4 slices bacon, crisp-cooked and crumbled
    ½ cup finely chopped green onions

slow cooker directions

1. Combine broth, turnip, lentils, onion, carrots, bell pepper, oregano and red pepper flakes in slow cooker.

2. Cover; cook on LOW 6 hours or on HIGH 3 hours or until lentils are tender.

3. Stir in olive oil and salt. Sprinkle with bacon and green onions.

prep time: 10 minutes • **cook time:** 6 hours (LOW) or 3 hours (HIGH)

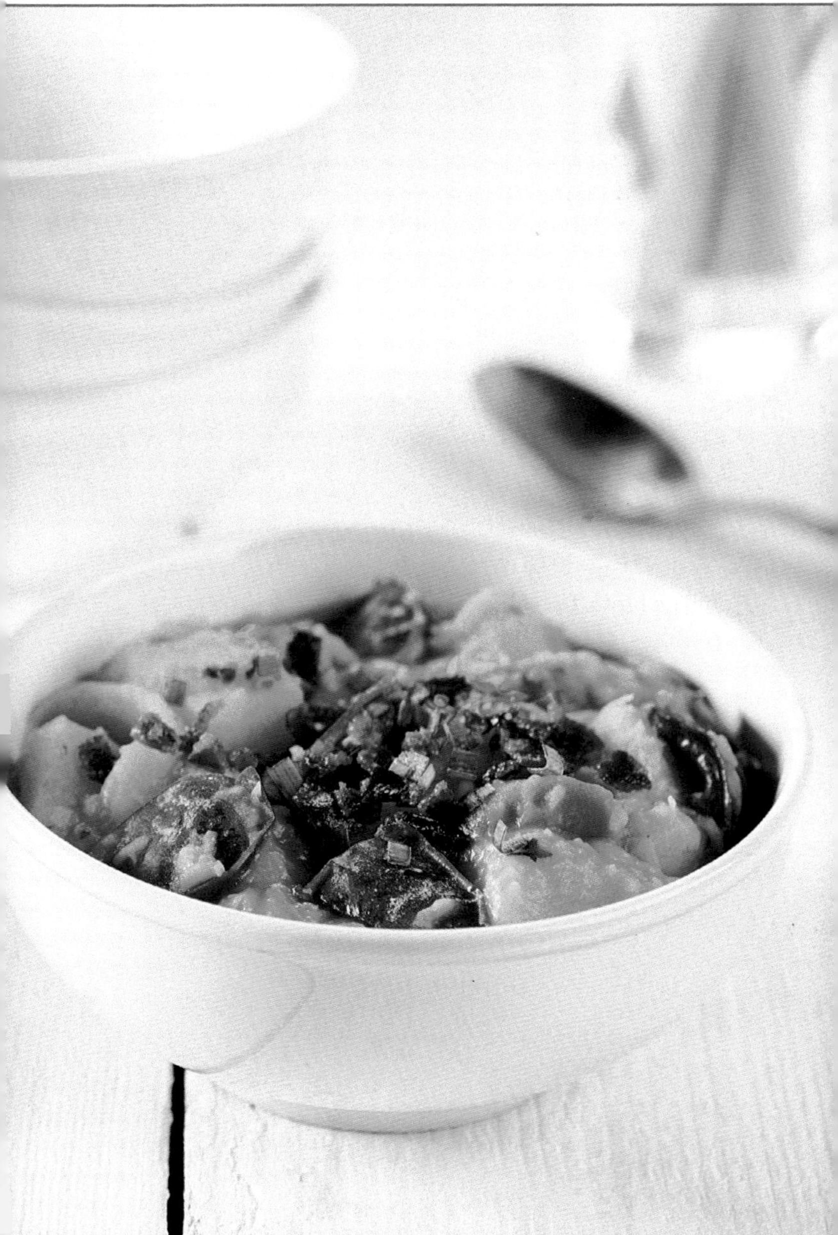

hearty mixed bean stew with sausage

makes 8 servings

³⁄₄ **pound sweet Italian pork sausage, casing removed**
10 **cups SWANSON® Chicken Stock**
¹⁄₄ **teaspoon ground black pepper**
2 **medium carrots, chopped (about ²⁄₃ cup)**
1 **stalk celery, chopped (about ¹⁄₂ cup)**
4 **ounces dried pinto beans (about ³⁄₄ cup)**
4 **ounces dried navy beans (about ³⁄₄ cup)**
4 **ounces dried kidney beans (about ³⁄₄ cup)**
6 **sun-dried tomatoes in oil, drained and thinly sliced (about ¹⁄₄ cup)**
  Grated Parmesan cheese

slow cooker directions

1. Cook the sausage in a 10-inch skillet over medium-high heat until it's well browned, stirring often to separate meat. Pour off any fat.

2. Stir the sausage, stock, black pepper, carrots, celery and beans in a 5-quart slow cooker.

3. Cover and cook on LOW for 7 to 8 hours.*

4. Stir in the tomatoes. Cover and cook for 1 hour or until the beans are tender. Sprinkle with the cheese.

Or on HIGH for 4 to 5 hours.

prep time: 15 minutes • **cook time:** 7 to 8 hours

acknowledgments

The publisher would like to thank the companies and organizations listed below for the use of their recipes and photographs in this publication.

Bob Evans®

Campbell Soup Company

Crystal Farms®

Del Monte Foods

Filippo Berio® Olive Oil

Hillshire Farm®

Hormel Foods, LLC

Jennie-O Turkey Store, LLC

National Fisheries Institute

Nestlé USA

Ortega®, A Division of B&G Foods, Inc.

The Quaker® Oatmeal Kitchens

Reckitt Benckiser LLC.

Riviana Foods Inc.

Tyson Foods, Inc.

Unilever

USA Dry Pea & Lentil Council

metric conversion chart

VOLUME MEASUREMENTS (dry)

¹/₈ teaspoon = 0.5 mL
¹/₄ teaspoon = 1 mL
¹/₂ teaspoon = 2 mL
³/₄ teaspoon = 4 mL
1 teaspoon = 5 mL
1 tablespoon = 15 mL
2 tablespoons = 30 mL
¹/₄ cup = 60 mL
¹/₃ cup = 75 mL
¹/₂ cup = 125 mL
²/₃ cup = 150 mL
³/₄ cup = 175 mL
1 cup = 250 mL
2 cups = 1 pint = 500 mL
3 cups = 750 mL
4 cups = 1 quart = 1 L

VOLUME MEASUREMENTS (fluid)

1 fluid ounce (2 tablespoons) = 30 mL
4 fluid ounces (¹/₂ cup) = 125 mL
8 fluid ounces (1 cup) = 250 mL
12 fluid ounces (1¹/₂ cups) = 375 mL
16 fluid ounces (2 cups) = 500 mL

WEIGHTS (mass)

¹/₂ ounce = 15 g
1 ounce = 30 g
3 ounces = 90 g
4 ounces = 120 g
8 ounces = 225 g
10 ounces = 285 g
12 ounces = 360 g
16 ounces = 1 pound = 450 g

DIMENSIONS

¹/₁₆ inch = 2 mm
¹/₈ inch = 3 mm
¹/₄ inch = 6 mm
¹/₂ inch = 1.5 cm
³/₄ inch = 2 cm
1 inch = 2.5 cm

OVEN TEMPERATURES

250°F = 120°C
275°F = 140°C
300°F = 150°C
325°F = 160°C
350°F = 180°C
375°F = 190°C
400°F = 200°C
425°F = 220°C
450°F = 230°C

BAKING PAN SIZES

Utensil	Size in Inches/Quarts	Metric Volume	Size in Centimeters
Baking or Cake Pan (square or rectangular)	8×8×2	2 L	20×20×5
	9×9×2	2.5 L	23×23×5
	12×8×2	3 L	30×20×5
	13×9×2	3.5 L	33×23×5
Loaf Pan	8×4×3	1.5 L	20×10×7
	9×5×3	2 L	23×13×7
Round Layer Cake Pan	8×1¹/₂	1.2 L	20×4
	9×1¹/₂	1.5 L	23×4
Pie Plate	8×1¹/₄	750 mL	20×3
	9×1¹/₄	1 L	23×3
Baking Dish or Casserole	1 quart	1 L	—
	1¹/₂ quart	1.5 L	—
	2 quart	2 L	—